Praise for Tom Stone

"Tom Stone has done somethi[...] his vast experience the simplest [...] und and lasting change in our lives [...] my own life and I am delighted th[...] es to help others on a large scale. I know his [...] have a positive impact on the lives of many, many people. I know [...] rough his pioneering work in Human Software Engineering he will accomplish this goal in a profound and powerful way."

—Jack Canfield, Co-author, *Chicken Soup for the Soul*® series and *The Success Principles*™: *How to Get from Where You Are to Where You Want to Be.*

"Tom Stone is nothing short of a genius. He is an expert in the area of dynamics, and he has the cleanest energy of ANYONE I've ever met, bar none. Even good coaches make an average of 20 coaching mistakes per session, but when I met with Tom, he made only one mistake—and then he immediately caught himself and corrected it! I was really amazed, and I immediately asked him to be my personal coach. I guess that makes him the coach to the coach to the coaches!"

—Thomas Leonard, Founder of *CoachVille* and Life Coaching Industry Pioneer

Praise for *Pure Awareness*

"The Pure Awareness Techniques that Tom Stone shares in this book have had a profound effect on my life. I became involved in the field of energy psychology early on and I believe that these methods can be used by every therapist, counselor, addiction specialist, life coach, and anyone who is interested in improving their life. I think you will be amazed and delighted at how rapid and simple these transformational tools are to practice."

—George J. Pratt, Ph.D., Chairman, Psychology, Scripps Memorial Hospital, La Jolla, Coauthor, *Instant Emotional Healing: Acupressure for the Emotions*

"I've used these techniques on a daily basis and continue to do so. As a result, today I experience a sense of continuous inner peace and connection with my Self."

—Colleen Moore, Licensed Marriage and Family Therapist, Auburn, CA

Praise for *Core Dynamics Coaching*

"After attending the Core Dynamics training in Phoenix, I threw away every other coaching strategy and tool I've ever learned because I don't need them anymore. People are coming from all over for appointments and are reporting transformations of mind-blowing proportions. There is no way to overstate the importance of the Core Dynamics training for coaching."

—Wendy Down, Master Certified Coach

"We may have come to some wrong conclusions in the past and the Core Dynamics method showed me how I could update my perspective to be more successful and effective both in business and in life. We often think that logic and intellect should be the only driver for business, but in the Core Dynamics Coach Training, I was shown how much power is available to us when we use all of who we are, including our emotions."

—Val Williams, Master Certified Coach

About the Author

Tom Stone is an internationally acclaimed coach and speaker, and an accomplished inventor, entrepreneur and writer. He has spent much of his life developing the most efficient and effective techniques for solving problems using principles and techniques from biophysics.

Tom is the pioneer of the new emerging field of Human Software Engineering (HSE) in which he has made a number of unique discoveries, including a set of profound insights into the nature of preverbal conditioning, called the Core Dynamics of Human Conditioning. This unique body of work provides the tools for easily eliminating the barriers and blocks that keep people from having the life they truly want.

Tom has turned his focus in recent years to finding effective solutions to many of the seemingly intractable problems that plague modern society, such as anxiety, depression and ADD/ADHD. This book is the culmination of several years of intensive research and is the first in the *Vaporize Your Problems* series. Tom lives in Carlsbad, California with his wife Lynda, where he directs his company, Great Life Technologies.

To learn more about Tom's work, please visit

www.greatlifetechnologies.com and
www.thepowerofhow.com

THE POWER OF

HOW

Simple Techniques to *Vaporize Your Ego* and *Your Pain-body*

Featuring
The 12 Core Dynamics of Human Conditioning &
The 8 Pure Awareness Techniques

TOM STONE

Foreword by Jack Canfield

The Power of How

Simple Techniques to Vaporize Your Ego and Your Pain-body
Featuring The 12 Core Dynamics of Human Conditioning &
The 8 Pure Awareness Techniques

By: Tom Stone
Foreword By: Jack Canfield

Published by:
Great Life Technologies, LLC
7040 Avenida Encinas, Suite 104 #380
Carlsbad, CA 92011
(619-557-2700
www.greatlifetechnologies.com

Magma font used throughout this book designed by Sumner Stone .

www.stonetypefoundry.com

To my wonderful wife Lynda

Acknowledgments

My heart felt thanks to all those who have contributed to my personal journey that has lead to the insights I am sharing here. The teachers and life experiences are too numerous to mention as every life experience has contributed in some way or another to bringing me to the knowledge of these wonderful Pure Awareness Techniques that I am sharing with you in this book.

I am grateful to my beautiful daughters Sharma and Serenity, for their love and support and for the great enrichment, insight and wisdom that having them in my life has brought me.

A very special thanks to Colleen Moore for the excellent editing of the manuscript and for suggesting the title – The Power of How. Another special thanks to Don Cramer for his additional editing. Thanks also to Gerri Ratigan for her contributions to the book cover and to Harold Riddle for the great job with the cover design and layout of the book. I greatly appreciate Cindy Tyler of Vervante for all of her help and support. I am deeply grateful to Robin Hill for his many contributions to so many things related to the book, the book web site, and to Great Life Technologies and handling so many things that freed my time so that I could write this book.

I also would like to express my deep appreciation to the team of people who provided valuable suggestions, feedback and other contributions to the book including Magi Speelpenning, Steve Straus, Patricia Coleman, Cathy Ellsmere, Gracia Wenzel, David Jakoby, Aimee Snow and Susan White. I'm also very grateful to Michelle LaPrise for her ideas and contributions.

I have an especially deep gratitude to Michael Stratford for his contribution to the special application of the GAP technique called SANYAMA and his delightful collaboration in teaching Core Dynamics Coach Training with me. I am also deeply grateful for the wonderful support of my work from Martin Keymer, Peter Barski, Wolfgang Bialas, Sandy Crow, Jo Ann Kilty, Leon Weiner, Sharon Velotas, Charmaine Briones, Adriana Bacelis, BarBara Whorley, Toni MacKenzie, Dr. Paul Jeong, Christian Mickelson, Drew Rozell, Paul Rarick, Michelle Humphrey, Cecelia Inwentarz, Mike Redfield, John Lingley, Rich Riedman, Melaney Gabris, Nancy Pagan, Donna Anderson, Tony Soto, Stephen Jones, Roger Hardie, Cora Whittington, Nancy Emmert, Martha Schutte, Pavla Kengelbacher, Aurora Winter, Sharon Yoon-kyung Noh, Aspen DeCew, Bob Brock, Wendy Down, and many, many others.

I am particularly grateful to all of my clients, seminar and training program participants, the Core Dynamics Coaches and Teachers, the WaveMaker Coaches and Human Software Engineers who have so whole heartedly embraced this work and who have provided an environment in which these techniques could be refined and perfected over the years. It is these pioneers of Human Software Engineering who are really propagating this work in the world. To all of you I offer my deepest gratitude.

I am very grateful to Oprah Winfrey for popularizing Eckhart Tolle's book The New Earth. The beautiful experiences of spiritual enlightenment that Eckhart describes in his books and Oprah's making the world aware of Eckhart's book have created an enormous wave of interest in people learning to truly free themselves from the limitations of their ego as well as free themselves from the stored emotional pain held in the "pain-body." This amazing world awakening has created a huge demand for more knowledge of "HOW" - How to resolve the pain in the pain-body quickly and completely - How to actually extract oneself from the identifications that create the ego. This awakened interest in learning how to truly live free of the ego and the pain-body needs simple, easy solutions that anyone can learn. As I have spent my life finding and refining exactly these simple, easy solutions, I am grateful for the enormous increased awareness of the need for them that Eckhart and Oprah have enlivened in the world. My deepest thanks to you both!

And I am grateful to you dear reader for opening these pages and for coming to this moment in your life in which you are on the threshold of learning some of the most important knowledge that you may ever come to know. May you use and enjoy these precious Pure Awareness Techniques, debug your ego and the pain held in your body and live and enjoy the totality of who and what you really are for the rest of your life!

Tom Stone
January 2009

Foreword

I was giving a seminar for a local business in Fairfield, IA, in December 1993. The company was using the large meeting room at the Fairfield Best Western Motel for the seminar. Tom Stone happened to be having lunch that day at the motel's restaurant called the Wild Rose. I was having lunch there as well with some of the participants from the seminar. A friend of Tom's was among them and as she and I were walking back from the salad bar, she stopped and introduced me to Tom.

"They tell me you are a walking miracle," I said. Less than five weeks before this Tom had been shot in the chest with a .44 caliber handgun by a stranger and had survived it. Now he was up and walking around, even having lunch at the restaurant. Tom's friend had already mentioned his incident to me. She had also told me a little bit about Tom's expert use of kinesiology also known as muscle testing. The three of us chatted and arranged for Tom to come to the motel that evening and give me a private session. I also invited Tom to join the group for the afternoon portion of my self-esteem seminar.

Tom did drop in for a while in the afternoon and learned that I was already very familiar with kinesiology. I had been intrigued with it for quite some time and often demonstrated its use in my classes.

That evening when Tom arrived, I only had an hour before I was going to be picked up and taken to another appointment so we quickly got started. My familiarity with muscle testing made me immediately comfortable with the process. As the session progressed, Tom quickly identified what was going on in me.

"What's bothering you?" he asked.

I want to affect the lives of a larger number of people. I want to help more people and have a bigger impact. I feel like I'm on a plateau that I am settling for less than I really want. We then spent some time discussing what it was that I wanted and crafting a positive intention statement. It read as follows:

"I have a major impact in the world, bringing love and empowerment to large numbers of people and I receive the natural benefits of this. I have the courage to take the necessary stands to manifest my vision."

We muscle tested me for this intention and I was "switched off." Tom explained that this indicated that there were "inner conflicts" that were blocking me from manifesting this intention as my reality.

Tom then proceeded to identify these inner conflicts. They ranged from areas of stress in my life having to do with money, to an earlier unpleasant experience, to unconscious ways that I was compensating for not getting the love I wanted, to limiting beliefs. I was amazed at the depth and scope of the issues that were blocking me. I was also fascinated with the incredible accuracy and speed with which Tom identified these patterns. I knew that muscle checking was a great tool, but I had never before seen it used in such a refined and precise manner.

The whole process took just about an hour. I was quite impressed. And I felt somehow different, like something inside had shifted. But would this really make a difference in my being able to broaden my influence and serve millions of people?

My first book, Chicken Soup for the Soul, was already written and published when I had that session with Tom. But it was only in the months that followed that the sales really started to take off and the book became the first in a series of best sellers. There are of course many other things that influenced this, but the simple procedures that Tom helped me with during that hour seemed to make a real difference between staying stuck in some old patterns and being able to break free and create what I really wanted for myself. One thing I vividly remember is that Tom "debugged" me for being a "packrat!" When I got home I cleaned out everything in my house and threw away literally about 15 garbage bags of accumulated unneeded stuff!

Since that time, Tom has truly become a master at using kinesiology to help people identify what is blocking them. He has worked with thousands of people helping them to clarify their life purpose, awaken their unique talents, and helping them remove their inner barriers to having the success in their lives that they truly want. Also in the intervening years he has been pioneering a whole new field that he calls Human Software Engineering™. It's about finding and fixing the "bugs" in our inner human software, and it is truly ground-breaking work.

In this brilliant book, The Power of HOW – Simple Techniques to Debug Your Ego and Your Pain-body, Tom has done something quite unique. He has distilled out of his vast experiences the simplest and most useful tools for creating profound and lasting change in your life. Even more importantly, he has identified exactly what to do to shift your old patterns of thoughts and feelings so that they no longer cause us to respond to life out of our old "knee jerk," conditioned responses. And if that weren't good enough, he has identified the essence of how to cultivate a whole new style of functioning that allows you to, as he says, "respond spontaneously to the needs of the moment with the fullness of your being." This is a potent combination and a whole new way of dismantling unwanted habits and limitation. It is unlike any other program for enriching your life that I've ever seen.

The unique thing about this book is that it is a practical guide that actually shows you how to really remove your inner barriers and conflicts. Lots of people have written about what you need to do to enjoy a better life; Tom actually gives you the tools for removing the things inside of you that keep tripping you up and getting in your way.

Recently I met with Tom and he showed me how to do the CORE Technique. Wow! I've done plenty of emotional release processing over the years but this was remarkably simple and especially deep and profound. I came out of something that had been nagging at me for weeks, and when it was complete, I felt a pervasive sense of bliss and expansion.

I am truly grateful to Tom for his help in my life and I am delighted that he is bringing his work out to share his insights and techniques to help others on a large scale. I know his desire is very similar to mine, to have a positive impact on the lives of many, many people. I know that through this book and Tom's pioneering work in creating Human Software Engineering he will accomplish this goal in a profound and powerful way.

Don't just read this book; actually do what it recommends and you will find your life changing in ways that will inevitably lead you to have a quality of life experience that is beyond your wildest dreams.

Jack Canfield

Co-author, Chicken Soup for the Soul® series and

The Success Principles™: How to Get from Where You Are to Where You Want to Be.

Contents

About the Author   iii

Acknowledgments   ix

Foreword   xiii

Preface   1

chapter 1
What's Missing in Most Spiritual Teachings?   5

chapter 2
What's Missing in Most Personal Development Programs?   15

chapter 3
The 12 Core Dynamics of Human Conditioning   27

chapter 4
Overview of the Eight Pure Awareness Techniques   55

chapter 5
The Pure Awareness Techniques   65

chapter 6
Pure Awareness Techniques Stories   211

chapter 7
Internet Resources   229

Appendix: The Essence of Each Core Dynamic   233

Preface

What you are about to learn will very likely be some of the most profound and important tools that you will ever learn in your life. These simple techniques can liberate you from the grip of emotion. They can bring you out of suffering. They can "debug" problems that you thought couldn't be solved. They can give you the experience of who and what you really are. They can connect you to your essential nature and to the essence of everything in the universe.

The Pure Awareness Techniques can give you the direct experience of what quantum physics calls the Unified Field. They can help you to live in the "zone" all the time. They can bring you out of inner conflicts and illusions. They can help you easily break habits that you have always wanted to break. They can save you from the grip of addictive behavior. They can bring you deep and lasting fulfillment that is more precious than any other accomplishment you'll have in your life.

And they are simple, easy to learn and easy to practice.

When using the Pure Awareness Techniques it doesn't take long to begin to liberate yourself from fear, anger, guilt, regret, resentment, depression, anxiety, worry, nervousness, and suffering, and to begin to experience more joy, fulfillment, success and happiness in your life than ever before.

These are big promises but they are easy to realize. It's not by reading the book that this will happen but by learning and practicing the techniques presented here. You only have to remember to use them. These simple techniques provide you with the quickest ways that

I have found to free yourself from suffering and problems. All you have to do is learn and practice the Pure Awareness Techniques in this simple book and all of this and more will be yours.

If you have read my first book, Pure Awareness – Five Simple Techniques for Experiencing Your Essential Nature, you will find much in The Power of How that is familiar. The Power of How is an expansion and revision of the first book. What has been added are detailed explanations of the three new Pure Awareness Techniques, SEE, SANYAMA and GPS as well as a summary of each of the 12 Core Dynamics and an explanation of the emerging field of Human Software Engineering. Other sections have been added as well on what's missing from most spiritual and personal development programs as well as other content. I know you will enjoy the revisions and the new techniques.

Enjoy Pure Awareness for it is the reality of what you truly are,

Tom Stone
January 2009
Carlsbad, California

chapter 1
What's Missing in Most Spiritual Teachings?

"I had a library of hundreds of hours of audio and video of Eckhart Tolle talking on the topics he discusses. I had listened and watched everything multiple times. I also had studied his books, and read them several times, but even with ALL of that, and as brilliant and articulate as Eckhart Tolle is, I was not able to effectively dismantle the habits which caused me to over-react or be reactive in general. With Tom Stone's Human Software Engineering approach I was able to shift patterns very quickly and I noticed my reactive tendencies were changing after only a few sessions. That was profound!"

— Paul Rarick

Mainly what most spiritual teachings lack are clear guidelines and techniques for simply, easily and directly experiencing your inner spiritual essence. Also typically missing or inadequate are guidelines and techniques for being able to rapidly remove the barriers to living from your inner spiritual essence all the time, which in the past has made true spiritual awakening a rare occurrence.

There are some wonderful books and seminars that describe genuine spiritual experiences but so often they don't tell you how to have these experiences yourself or how to cultivate a state in which

Pure Awareness, Pure Consciousness becomes a living reality for you instead of just a philosophical idea. In fact, having people get too absorbed in ideas about what spiritual experiences are like has a tendency to become a barrier in itself because you can become intellectually identified with "being spiritual."

The common themes, living life free of ego driven thinking and free of the emotional pain of the past are wonderful ideals to strive for. After all, who doesn't want to really know who they are and be free of suffering? (Well, some people might not be interested but if you're reading this book that's not you).

However, when those who have not yet had their own spiritual awakening read descriptions of spiritual awakening they are frequently left wondering – "How can I have such an experience myself?" "How can I gain the state of spiritual enlightenment and live in that state permanently?" "Is it possible for me to do that?" and "What do I have to do to have this become a reality for me?"

While the descriptions of the state of enlightenment in such books can be beautiful and inspiring, practical techniques for directly experiencing one's essential nature, one's own Pure Awareness are often not clearly presented. General guidelines may be provided, but specific step-by-step procedures based on a clear understanding of the true nature of the barriers to genuine spiritual experiences are missing. In addition, practical techniques for coming out of the grip of illusions caused by identification, expectation, attachment and unresolved emotional pain are usually missing. Without practical techniques that are simple and easy to learn and practice, the descriptions of spiritual enlightenment can actually be a source of frustration. Learning about how beautiful and liberating spiritual awakening is and not being able to easily get there oneself is discouraging.

It certainly seems that people do have spontaneous experiences of spiritual awakening. But when awakening happens by accident instead of by design the awakened person may be able to describe what he or she is experiencing but that doesn't mean that they understand how they got there. This often incomplete understanding of the mechanics of what gave rise to such an awakening frequently leads to generalized suggestions that most people simply can't follow in such a way as to produce a genuine awakening of their own. In essence, gaining spiritual enlightenment doesn't necessarily qualify you to help someone else also get there, not to mention get there quickly and easily.

What is needed is a set of tools for vaporizing the real barriers to living in a state of awakened consciousness all the time. That is precisely what this book is all about. I have spent the major portion of my adult life exploring and inquiring to find and develop just such practical spiritual techniques. After practicing Transcendental Meditation as taught by Maharishi Mahesh Yogi for more than 30 years, as well as many of Maharishi's advanced meditation techniques, I developed quite a deep familiarity with consciousness. But even with all of these many years of practicing meditation I would still at times get lost to the grip of emotional reactions and I was unable to sustain the experience of Pure Awareness all the time.

What I needed was a way to resolve my emotional reactions and the emotional pain from my past. We all have plenty of emotional pain from our past and I was no exception. Fortuitously in 1997 I discovered a simple technique for resolving emotional pain quickly and thoroughly that works almost like magic. For a few months I practiced this technique whenever I felt caught in the grip of an emotion. Then one evening as I was sitting in silence before reading my gratitude list, which was my habit at that time, I lingered in the silence for a little longer than usual and all of a sudden the sense of who I am shifted from Tom as an individual to the universality of Pure Awareness, unbounded consciousness.

As soon as this happened I found myself laughing and laughing at the huge cosmic joke that I had ever thought of myself as an isolated individual. I must have laughed for five minutes. The beautiful thing was that this shift was permanent. It has never gone away. I began to notice some extraordinary things as I started to live in this new state of being. I noticed that it became impossible to be judgmental about other people or myself. I didn't lose the ability to discern and distinguish; in fact this became greatly enhanced. I just found that whenever I began to consider being judgmental I would notice that what I was judging was something unresolved inside of me, so I would simply resolve it within myself and there would be no possibility of being judgmental.

I also noticed that anywhere that I went it felt like I was walking inside of a sea of my Self. Everything took on a kind of effortlessness and frictionless flow. I also felt a shift from needing to intellectually understand things to feeling and knowing things by simply experiencing them fully. I shifted from needing to understand the meaning of things with my mind to being completely at peace with simply knowing something from deep within myself without the need for intellectual understanding. I found that I began to perceive a kind of simple perfection in every experience. I was simply being present to everything just as it is. This all happened in the summer of 1997.

A few years prior to this I was speaking with a friend who had just returned from a trip to Switzerland. He was attending meetings with Maharishi and some of the teachers of meditation that Maharishi had trained who had themselves been practicing meditation for many, many years. My friend told me that someone asked Maharishi, "Maharishi, I've been meditating regularly for 25 years and I'm not feeling very enlightened. Why is that?" My friend said Maharishi answered this man and the whole group by saying, "You all have the consciousness, but you don't enjoy it, because of your habits. And you have to break those habits that are keeping you from enjoying the consciousness that you already have."

However, apparently Maharishi didn't have anything to say about what these habits are or how to break them. Just in that moment I had the clear sense that discovering what these habits are and the best and most efficient ways to break them was my life's purpose. It was my job to find out how to help people break the habits that keep them from enjoying the consciousness they already have. So that's what my life has been about for many years now and it appears that I have been successful at finding several simple guidelines and techniques for doing just that. That's what this book is about. It's about showing you how to break the habits that keep you from living and enjoying the consciousness that's already there. It's about showing you exactly how to rapidly cultivate a state in which you live and enjoy your essential nature – Pure Awareness, all the time.

As it turns out, this is much easier to do than it was thought to be in the past. In the past it was believed that it takes years or lifetimes of spiritual austerities and arduous practices to gain spiritual enlightenment. It also use to take months to cross the United States by ox cart. Only now we have new technologies for getting from New York to LA like the jet plane that make it fast and easy. And now new technologies of consciousness can make it much faster and easier to gain a fully awakened state of Pure Awareness than ever before.

What has been missing and needed are new insights into the nature of the habits that keep you locked in your illusions and then realistic, simple and practical tools for breaking these habits so that the reality of what you really are, the essential nature of what you truly are, Pure Awareness, can shine through, unobstructed in all its limitless peace and power. That's what this book is about. It's about the Power of How. The Power of How to debug the illusions that keep you in ignorance of your true self. The Power of How to debug your identifications that keep you absorbed in the illusion that you are your ego. The Power of How to extract your awareness from its habitual collapse inside of emotional reactions as a result of unmet expectations. The Power of How to debug the unresolved pain that you have stored in your "pain-body" as Eckhart Tolle puts it.

Without the simple, practical techniques for rapidly resolving your unresolved emotional pain and for rapidly extracting your awareness from your identifications, expectations, projections and habitual emotional reactions, the default way of life is to suffer and struggle. Most people live as the product of their conditioning. Most people live a life that is based on the avoidance of emotional pain. Most people do everything possible to self-medicate and numb out so that they don't have to feel the terrifying effects of being emotionally overwhelmed. They live inside the illusion that they are isolated individuals who are separate from the rest of life. You can't help but suffer and long for a sense of completion when you are lost to your illusions.

What I have discovered is that there are different ways to break the habits of being stuck in your illusions. Depending on the type of illusory state, there will be a different pathway back to the direct experience of Pure Awareness. There are eight Pure Awareness Techniques that I have discovered so far, each one useful for particular ways of regaining the direct experience of Pure Awareness when access to it has been lost under different circumstances.

There are two basic categories of barriers to living from Pure Awareness all the time. These are identifications and unresolved emotional pain. This is important enough that I'll repeat it. There are two basic categories of barriers to living from Pure Awareness all the time:

- Identifications – getting part of the sense of who you are from things that are not who you really are.

- Unresolved Emotional Pain – patterns of energy held in the body that are incomplete experiences from the past.

When you successfully debug your identifications and emotional pain you are free. Then you live in a natural state of freedom and bliss and never lose the presence of Pure Awareness. There's nothing left to block it. It's already there. Your awareness is present all the time. Its presence makes it possible for you to even be reading these words. But because you are typically so absorbed in your experiences and so filled with identifications and unresolved emotional pain you don't experience and enjoy living the conscious presence of your own essential nature, Pure Awareness.

The good news is that there are only a finite number of these inner barriers keeping you from living and enjoying Pure Awareness all the time. And with the simple Pure Awareness Techniques that you will learn in this book and from the audio files of demonstrations of them that you can listen to via the Internet, you'll soon be identifying your own inner barriers and vaporizing them at every opportunity to do so.

Many spiritual teachings involve generic practices that very gradually cultivate more and more awareness. This is fine and it works but it can be very slow. Some people practice such techniques their whole lives and still don't experience the full awakening of their consciousness.

The main thing that distinguishes the Pure Awareness Techniques from these generic spiritual practices is that we specifically target those inner barriers that block the direct experience of Pure Awareness and resolve them. This is what makes this approach so fast. This is why people begin to report within just one or two years of diligently practicing these techniques that they predominantly live in the state of Pure Awareness all the time.

It's not just gaining this state of awakening that's important. It is also important to continue to use the techniques to enrich the enjoyment of your awakened state more and more. Even after you shift from the sense of yourself coming from your ego to the sense of what you are as being the Totality, being able to fully enjoy this state will be enhanced more and more by the continued use of the Pure

Awareness Techniques throughout your life.

Another reason why many spiritual teachings are ineffective in providing genuine spiritual experiences is that the teaching has lost connection with directly experiencing the essential nature of life as one's own Pure Awareness and only the superficial shell of the original spiritual teaching remains. Time has a way of degrading things. As the original knowledge gets passed down from one generation to the next, the purity and efficacy of it can gradually be lost.. What often remains are codes of behavior, dogma and rituals that are pursued with passion by devotees with deep belief that what they are doing is going to bring them true spiritual awakening. But sometimes the real essence of the practice has been lost and no one really knows what it was.

Here's an example. A commonly held belief in many spiritual traditions is that in order to gain spiritual enlightenment it is necessary to renounce worldly life and become a reclusive monk or nun. The idea is that being involved in the material world interferes with spirituality. Where does this idea come from? It comes from misinterpretations of ancient descriptions of the state of Pure Awareness. In different traditions ancient texts say that in the state of Pure Awareness there are no desires. As you will see when you experience Pure Awareness while using the GAP Technique this is perfectly true. There are no desires in Pure Awareness. In fact, there is nothing but awareness itself. In order to have a desire you have to have both a desirer and something to be desired. In the state of Pure Awareness there is nothing being perceived so there are no objects of experience and therefore there is nothing there for which one can have a desire.

However, when someone who has not experienced Pure Awareness reads the description of it as being a state in which there are no desires, they can mistake the description of the state for the method of getting there. They have mistaken the ends for the means. This leads to the notion that it is necessary to get rid of desires in order to experience your inner spiritual essence. So people abandon worldly life and become reclusive attempting to give up their desires in hopes of attaining Pure Awareness. This is an unfortunate misinterpretation of the ancient texts. The enlightened authors of these texts were simply describing an attribute of their experience of being in the state of Pure Awareness not explaining how to get there.

There are many such mistaken notions about what it takes to gain true spiritual experiences and to maintain the presence of Pure Awareness all the time. When a practice is a misinterpretation or when it is something that once had power and truth in it but has lost its purity over time then the practice becomes slow and ineffective. This has discouraged most people from being interested in seeking spiritual enlightenment. Few people have the discipline or tenacity to practice techniques that are difficult and that take a long time to produce the desired result. You have to be extremely dedicated or maybe even a little nuts to do that. But in the absence of effective ways to directly experience Pure Awareness and effective techniques that quickly bring about a permanent state of living in Pure Awareness, what else was there to do? As you are about to discover, experiencing Pure Awareness is incredibly simple and easy. There are no austerities needed. No renunciation. After all it is perfectly possible that the ascetic can still be attached to his loincloth and cave. Giving up worldly life isn't a guarantee of getting you there, in fact if may be a distraction.

chapter 2
What's Missing in Most Personal Development Programs?

"I had spent 14 years in personal development—I read over 100 books, and attended countless seminars. At one point, I attempted to add up how much I spent and it was over $120,000 in my search to "find me." But I always felt there was still something missing. Through learning and practicing the Pure Awareness Techniques I feel like I hit the jackpot."

"I have completed and permanently moved through all those inner conflicts; I have let go of the stories and over identifications and I now feel free, alive, more aligned with my life and back in love with my life. Other teachings come close; but NOTHING is so simple, precise and gives you immediate results like the Pure Awareness Techniques that Tom so masterfully teaches."

– Michelle Humphrey

The way I describe the process of identifying and removing the inner barriers to living from Pure Awareness all the time is to use a computer analogy. I describe it as learning how to debug and upgrade yourself. I call it Human Software Engineering sometimes referred to simply as HSE. Over and over again my students tell me that Human Software Engineering provides the missing and much needed ingredients that are lacking in most personal development programs.

Many personal development programs will tell you what actions to take in order to have the life you want. But when people attempt to do these things they usually fall back into their previous conditioned ways of functioning, often without even realizing that this is happening. What's missing is how to actually remove the influences that cause you to slip back into your ineffective conditioned ways of being. How to remove these insidious influences is exactly what the Power of How is all about.

For example, many people have been excited about the book and movie called "The Secret" that teaches about a natural law referred to as "The Law of Attraction." The Law of Attraction is an observation that whatever you put your attention on tends to manifest in your life. You attract that which you think about. So the idea is to think about only that which you really want and not think about the negative self-sabotaging thoughts that often accompany people's desire, goals and dreams.

When people attempt to make practical use of the Law of Attraction they often say that it doesn't work because they aren't getting what they intended. Actually it is working, it's just that it's working not only on the thoughts about what you really want, it's also working on all of the contrary thoughts and feelings that arise as a result of your conditioning.

What's missing are techniques for being able to eliminate those thoughts and feelings that come up from your conditioning. These thoughts and feelings don't just go away because you decide that they should. Like a virus on your computer, self-sabotaging thoughts and feelings corrupt your "output" so you don't get what you thought you wanted, you get the sum of what you want combined with your conditioned self-sabotaging thoughts and feelings.

Here's how it works. Physics has clearly identified that everything is made of energy. Matter is made of molecules. Molecules are made of atoms. Atoms are made of subatomic particles and subatomic particles we now know are made up of waves of energy. That means that everything is made of energy. This is also true for non-physical things like thoughts, feelings, desires, conditioning, basically... everything is made of energy.

So, say you have a desire such as, "I want a new car." This desire may immediately be followed by a thought that comes from your conditioning such as, "But I don't have the money." Or "I probably won't qualify for financing." "I guess I'll just go wash the old one." The energy of the intention to get a new car crashes head on with the conditioned negating thoughts and the energy of the original intention gets canceled out. Looked at from the perspective of physics, self-sabotage is a simple matter of one wave of energy interfering with and canceling out another wave of energy. Here's what it looks like if we graph one cycle of the crest and trough of a wave of energy of an intention juxtaposed with one wave of energy of a conditioned negating thought.

The Physics of Inner Conflicts

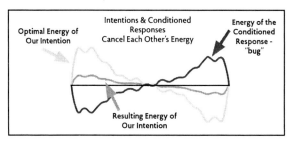

Starting from the left, the line on the top represents one cycle of the waveform of the energy of our intention such as, "I want to get a new car." The line on the bottom represents the energy of our contrary self-sabotaging thought or feeling such as, "Oh, I probably can't afford it." The line in the middle is the sum of the top and bottom lines (the result of their interference with each other) and it represents the net result of having both kinds of thoughts. It is what's left of the energy of our original intention to get the new car. What happens? We don't even bother to begin to process of looking for the new car. It stops right there. There's just not enough energy to support the action so nothing happens.

I like to think of the Law of Attraction as a mechanism for setting in motion everything that is needed to bring about that which we think. To playfully dramatize this and the phenomena of having our intentions sabotaged by our conditioned responses, imagine that there are a bunch of little gnomes who are responsible for organizing all of the details of the manifestation of your thoughts. Just imagine that when you say or think the thought that you want a new car, the little gnomes (who can read your mind) come running out of their little houses and start scurrying around to organize the new car for you. That's their job.

But when you have the conditioned negating thoughts right afterwards, the little gnomes throw up their hands in disgust and say, "He didn't mean it. Forget it. Let's go home." And they walk back into their little houses shaking their heads.

The result – no new car!

So the problem is how to get rid of the conditioned negating thoughts that are sabotaging what it is that you really want. The conditioned sabotaging thoughts don't go away just because you want them too. As long as the negating thoughts and feelings are not being properly and effectively handled you will continue to get the combined results of your intentions and your conditioned responses. The laws of physics, the interaction of the energy of your intentions with the energy of your conditioned responses is going to happen. That's how the laws of nature work. Without learning how to remove the invisible self-sabotaging influences of your conditioning you will basically continue to get about what you have now.

Some personal development teachers understand that it is the influence of our conditioning that is in the way of manifesting what we truly want. They understand that our conditioning sabotages our intentions. They even say that you need to overcome your conditioning. But the vast majority of people don't know how to do that. In fact it would appear that most personal development programs either don't offer solutions or the solutions are not very effective, are too difficult or the instructions to generalized and not clear enough to be truly applicable and useful. People may get some benefit from such programs but many are left with the feeling that something is missing. They are inspired but they don't quite know what to do to thoroughly overcome the conditioning.

If you think you can avoid conditioning consider this. Think of a time when you were young and you noticed something about your parents that you didn't like. Can you remember swearing to yourself that you would never be like that? Now that you are grown up yourself you probably have had the realization at some point that you have been doing the same behavior that your parents did. Conditioning is powerful. It's insidious. Most of the time you don't know that it is happening and even if you did you would not be able to shield yourself against its influence. Conditioning is a basic part of what happens to us as humans.

What is possible though is to learn new techniques that can help you to extract yourself from the limitations produced by your conditioning. To be effective this means that you'll need to learn to do some things that are the opposite of what you've been doing by default. The Pure Awareness Techniques that you will be learning in this book are exactly this. They will teach you with clear, simple guidelines exactly what to do to remove the limitations caused by your conditioning so that you can begin to operate in completely new ways. You will become a different person. You will become someone who functions not as the product of your conditioned responses but from the clarity and awareness of your essential nature, Pure Awareness.

Removing the Limiting Influences of Your Conditioning

What is needed in both spiritual teachings and personal development programs are techniques to solve problems created by the limiting influences of your conditioning. To do this you need to know what your conditioning is, where it comes from, and most importantly, what to do to remove its invisible self-sabotaging influences. Providing these missing elements to solve the problems of your conditioning is exactly what this book is about.

The emerging field of Human Software Engineering creates a new context for solving these problems. Rather than attempting to solve problems with the intellect, we must take an experiential approach. This is because the conditioning that causes so many problems did not originate from the intellect, and therefore doesn't exist at the level of the intellect. This is why conventional therapy and coaching often fall short in solving problems because practitioners attempt to solve problems using the intellect. The field of Human Software Engineering approaches problems as simply patterns of energy and information. In this approach, problems and conditioned responses are seen as "viruses" or "bugs" in our "inner human software." With a Human Software Engineering approach we ask, "Why can't we simply run some anti-virus software on our inner human software and 'debug' and 'upgrade' it so that we can have the output that we really want?" Well, that's precisely what we are going to do. You'll be learning just how to debug and upgrade your own personal inner human software so that your conditioning stops sabotaging your desires. An important part of Human Software Engineering is the understanding of the real nature of our conditioning, how we got it and what it does to us. This understanding is provided by the penetrating insights of the Core Dynamics of Human Conditioning Model. Most importantly, the methods for removing the insidious influences of our conditioning are provided by the eight Pure Awareness Techniques. I'll start by giving you an introduction to the principles of Human Software Engineering. Then we'll look specifically at the insights about the nature of our conditioning provided by the Core Dynamics of Human Conditioning Model. Then the majority of the book is about how to actually do the Pure Awareness Techniques that will liberate you from the limitations of your conditioning.

The Pure Awareness Techniques taught in this book are organized into four basic groups:

1. How to experience Pure Awareness

    - GAP
    - AGAPE

2. How to debug your identifications and thus your ego

    - SEE
    - WONDER

3. How to cultivate a state of pure knowing and certainty

    - SANYAMA
    - WAIT

4. How to debug the unresolved emotional pain stored in your body

    - CORE
    - GPS

Direct Experience Rather Than Just Intellectual Understanding

Intellectual understanding about spiritual awakening is wonderful but having an understanding of what living in a state of enlightenment is like doesn't produce the actual state of enlightenment. If anything, it complicates it by getting you too caught up in thinking about it rather than having the direct experience of it. In order to really know anything you must first directly experience it.

Consider for a moment the taste of a strawberry. If you had never tasted one, and yet you had a detailed explanation of what a strawberry tasted like, (sweet, juicy, tart, etc.) would the description provide you with real knowledge of what a strawberry tastes like? Of course not! You have to take a bite. Only when you have actually tasted a strawberry can you really be an authority on how it tastes.

Similarly, without the taste of Pure Awareness - without the taste of awakened consciousness - all the descriptions in the world of what enlightenment is like will not give you the real knowledge of it. That's why I'm not going to bother with detailed descriptions of the experience of Pure Awareness until you have tasted it. I do believe, however, that you need an orientation to the basis of the Pure Awareness Techniques and an orientation about what keeps you from having direct experiences of Pure Awareness. This orientation will cover:

- An introduction to the new field of Human Software Engineering.

- An overview of the 12 Core Dynamics of Human Conditioning - a set of penetrating insights into the nature of preverbal human conditioning that keep you from experiencing and living in Pure Awareness. This model is our roadmap of the barriers to living in Pure Awareness all the time.

- An overview of the eight Pure Awareness Techniques.

Human Software Engineering: How to Debug and Upgrade Your Inner Human Software

Since the mid 1990's I have been pioneering a new field called Human Software Engineering. Human Software Engineering (HSE) is based on the idea that we created computers to automate certain human tasks and so therefore they behave in many ways like we do and vice versa. This means that by using computer software analogies we can gain new insights about ourselves. In HSE we talk about "debugging" and "upgrading" our inner human software. We describe the inner barriers that block us from having the life that we want as the "bugs" in our inner human software. The use of personal computers has become so widespread that it makes the use of the computer analogy something everyone understands.

Working with thousands of people in my development of HSE, I learned that it was   important to identify and understand the real nature of things that block us from experiencing Pure Awareness all the time. I began and continued over many years, a penetrating inquiry into the nature of these inner barriers. What I discovered as I kept looking deeper and deeper was the real foundation of our inner barriers. I found that the specific barriers to experiencing Pure Awareness all the time are of two kinds:

- Identifications
- Incomplete emotional experiences

Both of these inner barriers are kinds of bugs in our inner human software. They are based in very early, pre-verbal childhood conditioning. Pre-verbal childhood conditioning is one major category of bugs in our inner human software.

As I explored the nature of our early conditioning it became increasingly obvious that we have lots of pre-verbal experiences that we of course were not able to categorize with words. Instead we experienced them directly. However, it also seems that we tend to make "feeling level decisions" about ourselves and about the world around us based on these experiences. These "feeling level decisions" are made without words and they form a set of profound limitations on what we allow ourselves to experience. Feeling level decisions also cultivate the habits of acquiring both false identifications and incomplete emotional experiences, thus forming the ego and pain-body.

Human Software Engineering not only includes the penetrating insights of the Core Dynamics of Human Conditioning and the Pure Awareness Techniques, but also includes other techniques for debugging and upgrading our inner human software. I have found that there are several categories of "bugs" in our inner human software and that our conditioning is only one of the categories. There are other kinds of bugs such as ones that are inherited from previous generations, bugs caused by electromagnetic fields of pathogens, toxins, allergens, etc. But these are other stories for other books. Right now we are exploring those aspects of HSE that are specifically about the debugging and upgrading of our inner human software to be able to live in permanent Pure Awareness.

chapter 3

The 12 Core Dynamics of Human Conditioning

The Origin of Problems

There are many forms of preverbal conditioning, and the main ones, summarized on a chart below, are called the Core Dynamics of Human Conditioning. An expanded Venn diagram is used to show the interrelationships between each of these Core Dynamics.

The Core Dynamics of Human Conditioning

Each Core Dynamic is the expression of a "feeling-level decision" that we made when we were very young. These decisions were not made with words. They are preverbal and precognitive. When we grow up and acquire verbal and cognitive skills, we forget that we made these powerful, wordless feeling-level decisions. But the influence of these decisions persists. We continue to live inside of their limiting influences.

On the diagram the three central Core Dynamics - Trying to Force an Outcome, Looking for Yourself Where You Are Not and Resisting Feeling Things Fully - form the "operating system level" of our bugged inner human software. Each of these three central Core Dynamics has three primary expressions shown in the corresponding expanded oval. The corresponding nine Core Dynamics are considered our "office suite" of bugged application software.

The Core Dynamics model is a road map of the nature of our pre-verbal conditioning. In order to understand how preverbal conditioning affects us, it will be useful to take a look at the basic structure of all human experiences.

The Three Aspects of Every Human Experience

Every human experience is composed of three fundamental components: The person having the experience, or the experiencer, the object of experience, and the process of experiencing. For example, if you take a bite of a strawberry, you are the experiencer, the strawberry is the experience, and your senses (in this case all five senses: taste, touch, smell, sight and hearing) are involved. Together, these three aspects of experiencer, object of experience and process of experiencing are essential to all of our experiences.

As we've discussed, when we are very young we have experiences that are too much for our delicate systems to process. Our mechanisms of experiencing are not yet developed enough to handle many of our experiences prior to developing language. So as a result, we tend to become inappropriately identified with a mistaken interpretation of one or more of the three components of experience. And this is where problems begin.

If we identify too strongly with the object of our experience, we tend to develop the sense that some crucial part of ourselves is missing. If we identify too strongly with our notions of who we think we are (the experiencer), we tend to develop the sense that we are our ego, the composite of the stories about who we think we are. If we identify too strongly with the process of experiencing, we will often end up being easily overwhelmed and afraid to feel things fully. As the diagram that follows shows, identifying too strongly with any one of the three aspects keeps us from experiencing a sense of being whole, and of feeling things fully. We will be cut off from Pure Awareness, without being aware of this of course.

These three aspects of every experience are not independent. They all exist together. However, when the predominance of identification becomes emphasized between any two of them we experience frustration, struggle and isolation. For example, if we tend to identify strongly both with a false sense of ourselves and with the object of our experience, we end up feeling frustration, because we are completely identified with our ego and at the same time feel strongly that some part of ourselves is missing. If we identify too strongly both with our false inner sense of self and the process of experiencing, we end up feeling like we're in constant struggle, because the ego, which demands that its presence be recognized, is battling against the temptation to become absent in the face of strong emotions. If, on the other hand, we tend to over-identify with the object of our experience and the process of experiencing, we can feel terribly isolated, since we at once feel as though some part of ourselves is not there and we feel terrified of being overwhelmed.

The Origin of Problems

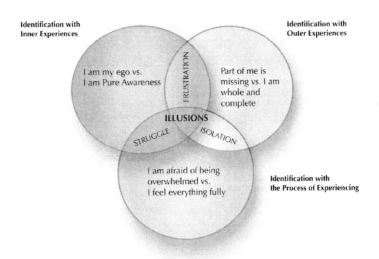

You can probably relate to the feelings I just described in the last paragraph. And whether you have become identified with one, two or all three of these components of human experience, you'll tend to remain stuck, unable to become truly aware of the wholeness of your experiences. You'll suffer under illusions, helpless to change things.

When we are very little we make decisions about ourselves and about our experience of the world around us even though we cannot yet express these decisions with language. These rudimentary decisions form the basis of our preverbal conditioning. Since language is not yet available to us—or is at the most very under developed—these decisions are made at the level of feeling. Language we may not have, but feelings we have in abundance. And it is these feeling level decisions that become the basis of the 12 Core Dynamics of Human Conditioning.

Understanding the nature of our preverbal conditioning by understanding the essence of each of the 12 Core Dynamics sheds light on exactly how our conditioning operates to keep us absorbed and lost inside the grip of our life experiences. This understanding also helps us to begin to appreciate the invisible, unconscious quality of the conditioning. In addition, it helps us to understand when and why to use the eight Pure Awareness Techniques as the antidotes to being caught up in and lost to our illusions that the Core Dynamics create. The following is a description of the basic insights into the nature of the conditioning of each of 12 Core Dynamics of Human Conditioning.

The Core Dynamics

Resisting Feeling Things Fully

This Core Dynamic is based on the experience of being emotionally overwhelmed when we are very young and making a feeling level decision to attempt to not feel intense emotional experiences fully. It was the best response to our fear of emotional overwhelm that we could come up with at the time and it seems to be universal. In other words, everyone seems to make this preverbal decision. It just seems to come with the territory of being human. The consequences of making this feeling level decision are that we begin to build our life around strategies of feeling avoidance in order to minimize the awful experience of being emotionally overwhelmed.

The three primary expressions of these strategies that are also feeling level decisions in and of themselves are:

- Ignoring Your Intuition
- Being Judgmental
- Avoiding the Present

Ignoring Your Intuition

Just about everyone has experienced having intuitive insights and then not consistently trusting and acting on them. It is only later when you discover that your intuition was right you could just kick yourself for not acting on it. Why do we do not trust and act on our intuition consistently?

After the feeling level decision to resist feeling things fully is already in place, we have all kinds of experiences of doing things to explore life, our bodies and the world around us. Sometimes these explorations meet with resistance from our parents or others. For example if we draw a picture all over our bedroom wall with a felt-tip marker, we might be excited to share our creative self-expression with our parents but they may not share our enthusiasm for what we have done. If we get punished for it we may experience an array of overwhelming emotions such as feeling betrayed, bewildered, hurt, scared, fearful and angry that our source of love, support and nurturing has turned on us. What could be more terrifying? And we have yet another experience of being emotionally overwhelmed.

It doesn't take having many experiences like this before we start to have the fear of negative consequences that will lead to emotional overwhelm immediately following any intuitive or creative impulse that may come to us. This cultivates the habit of NOT trusting or acting on our intuition. It also creates confusion as to what is our intuition and what is not. In addition, it cultivates the fear of confrontation, the fear of standing up for yourself, the fear of being true to yourself, the fear of expressing your creativity, especially under any circumstances where there's the possibility of someone being upset with us for what we do.

Being Judgmental

Most of us grow up in an environment in which people are judgmental of themselves and others. We learn to do this by observation of this behavior modeled by others. But there's more to it than that. The phenomenon of being judgmental is a way of resisting feeling things fully. Sometimes we have a feeling inside of ourselves that we don't want to feel, something that makes us feel uncomfortable. We can have a feeling like this triggered by seeing someone who is displaying a behavior that is similar to a behavior of our own that is associated with our own discomfort.

It is easier to see it in someone else. It is also easier to judge it as something bad or wrong in them rather than admit that this is also something inside of us. We don't want to feel the feeling of our own discomfort with our own behavior so we develop a tendency to express our distaste, our judgmental feelings, toward or about the other person or situation rather than feeling the feeling inside of ourselves. The charge that is the energy of being judgmental is however inside of us, not over there in the other person. Whether we are judging someone else or judging a part of ourselves, the result is the same; we use it as a strategy so that we don't have to feel strong overwhelming feelings that are inside of us.

It is the entire phenomenon of avoidance of our own inner feelings of discomfort through being judgmental that is modeled for us. Just watching this behavior conditions us to adopt it too. After all, it seems to us like being judgmental is just a part of how people are.

Avoiding the Present

When we resist feeling things fully we have a tendency to not complete intense emotional experiences. In our attempt to avoid emotional overwhelm we archive the residue of these unresolved intense emotional experiences. This causes us to accumulate a database of patterns of unresolved, incomplete emotional energy in our bodies. It's called "emotional baggage" or the pain-body. Everyone has it in varying degrees. This is because the Core Dynamic of *Resisting Feeling Things Fully* is so universal.

The result of having a database of incomplete emotional energies held in our body is that when we allow ourselves to be fully present, the patterns of energy of the incomplete experiences begin to press into our awareness demanding to be felt and completed. The body seems to have an innate intelligence of wanting to be free of the stress and tension caused by holding the incomplete emotional energy inside. But we don't want to feel these feelings. We're afraid of being overwhelmed by them so we adopt behaviors of avoiding the present so that we don't have to face this fear or experience the residual emotional pain from the past. This leads to the use of mood-altering substances and all kinds of addictive behaviors in order to self-medicate to avoid the pain. This is the real underlying basis of addictions. Some of these addictions can be as simple as absorbing ourselves in stories about the past or the future just to stay out of the present where the potential of having to face and feel the pain of the past seems like a dangerous thing to do. Other strategies include such things as smoking, drinking, over-eating, the use of both illicit drugs and prescription drugs, and a whole host of behaviors all designed to avoid the present so that we don't have to feel the stored pain of the past.

Looking For Yourself Where You Are Not

This conditioning occurs within the first days and weeks after we are born. While we are in the womb we don't have the experience of having needs because they are all met automatically. Pardon the pun but I refer to this as - Five Star Womb Service! When we come out and the umbilical cord is cut, now we experience needs. We need nourishment. We need our diaper changed. We need warmth and love and burping! And mom still feels like a part of us even after the umbilical cord is cut. She feels like the part of us that meets our needs.

We have the combination of our complete dependence on others for getting our needs met and being identified with our mother. This combination of dependence and identification makes us feel that when a need doesn't get met quickly enough rather than saying, "Hey, where's mom? This is awful! She's not meeting my need. I don't know if I'll survive if my need doesn't get met" we make a feeling level conclusion that it is a part of ourselves that is missing. Of course we don't have language yet and we don't even have the distinction of mom as a separate being. After all, we were just inside of her for nine months and it still feels like she is an extended part of ourselves that meets our needs. We interpret the experiences of our needs not getting met by making the feeling level decision that – part of me is missing – and it's the part of me that meets my needs.

This again seems to be quite universal. Having our needs not met in a timely way happens even in the best of households. It seems that everyone develops the tendency to feel like a part of himself or herself is missing to one degree or another. This leads to a pervasive feeling that if I could just get my needs met then I'd finally feel whole and complete. So we chase after goals and desires with an undercurrent of hope that when the goal is reached or the desire is fulfilled that this will finally make us feel whole and complete.

But the problem is that no amount of love, attention, money, time, possessions, experiences, no amount of anything, can possibly make us feel whole and complete. This is because we already are whole and complete so there's nothing missing to begin with. But it doesn't FEEL like we're whole. It feels like we won't be whole and complete unless we get the right romantic partner, or the perfect job, or the sports car or the house with an ocean view. When we reach these goals, expecting these accomplishments and acquisitions to bring us lasting fulfillment, how long does the sense of fulfillment actually last? Not very long! This is because there isn't anything that can satisfy this longing for a sense of completion but we keep trying, thinking that the next thing will finally do it for us. What's really missing is the direct experience of what we really are, our essential nature – Pure Awareness. What is needed is to directly experience that we are already whole and complete. As you'll soon see, the experience of Pure Awareness provides the very experience of being whole and complete that we've been longing for all of our lives.

The Core Dynamic - Looking For Yourself Where You Are Not - gives rise to its three primary expressions:

- Mistaking Need For Love
- Resisting Change
- Limiting Self-expression

Mistaking Need For Love

Due to the nature of the Core Dynamic of Looking For Yourself Where You Are Not we are so intent on making sure that our needs get met that the meeting of needs becomes confused with the experience of love. In truth however, getting a need met is simply getting a need met. It doesn't really have anything to do with love. We become conditioned to think that love means getting needs met. "If you loved me you would ..." (meet my need). But feeling loved is just a variation on feeling whole and complete. Love is actually more of a state of being than it is something that you give or get from others.

Advertisers use this confusion all the time. Need, attachment and identification are all marketed to us under the false label of love. If you just buy this nice perfume, you'll attract the man of your dreams. Ad copy writers intuitively know that people don't distinguish between love and need and they cleverly play on this to motivate you to buy something. Your motivation is that you are lead to feel that if you purchase this product you will get your need met and you will finally feel loved.

When you experience Pure Awareness you are experiencing a state of pure love. It is the only thing that truly is love; it is unconditional love. That means that love isn't dependent upon anything outside of you. You naturally love unconditionally by simply being in the state of pure love that is the same as Pure Awareness. The only true form of love is unconditional. Everything else is need.

Resisting Change

We all want to have a stable, secure and safe foundation for our lives. As such, we like to have things that we can depend upon, things that don't change. However, there isn't anything in creation that isn't changing even if the changes are sometimes imperceptible. What we are really looking for (usually without knowing it) is the only real unchanging state of being that exists. That state of being – Pure Awareness - is the unchanging nature of our own inner essence. As you will see when using the GAP Technique, Pure Awareness is unchanging. There's nothing there to change. You need duality and diversity to have change. In Pure Awareness there is only Awareness itself. Pure Awareness is the only stable unchanging reference that it is possible to have. And using the Pure Awareness Techniques you can rapidly cultivate a state of being in which the awareness of Pure Awareness is always present and never lost. This is the only real state of stability that is possible.

In the absence of the experience of Pure Awareness what happens is that we do a special form of Looking For Yourself Where You Are Not. We become identified with things in our lives that SEEM like they are not changing. We become attached and identified with anything that has simply been around for a long time. Our old unresolved emotional pain can have this quality of feeling. In fact anything that seems like it's been around for a long time can become a source of identification; your job or career (if you had it for a long time), your name, your status or degree, your body, your reputation, your home, spouse or children, your habits and conditioning, your ideology or beliefs or religion. But none of these are things that are truly non-changing. These things are all subject to change and to the degree that you are getting part of the sense of yourself from any of them, you will resist change in order to protect your sense of self.

Limiting Self Expression

If part of the sense of who we are is coming from the feeling of being connected to our friends and family and if most of these people are not powerfully self-expressed in the world (which is usually the case) then we may have a tendency to hold ourselves back from being fully self-expressed in the world ourselves. We will unknowingly participate in a game that we might call – "Let's all stay mediocre together!" This Core Dynamic, Limiting Self Expression, is an expression of Looking

For Your Self Where You Are Not because it causes us to NOT start that new business or NOT write that book we've been meaning to write, etc. Limiting Self Expression also tends to keep us from living from Pure Awareness all the time because we are identified with the false sense that our connection with others, having them like us, accept us, or approve of us is something that we can't afford to be without.

Limiting Self Expression also expresses itself as the fear that others, even people we don't know, will disapprove of us or our creative expression. We're afraid that people will take pot shots at us. "What if they don't like my book?" "What if someone criticizes my creative expression?" "I'll just hold back and not put it out there and then I don't have to be at risk."

Strangely enough the reason that people don't want us to be powerfully self-expressed or successful is that it puts it in their face that they are playing small. Our powerful self-expression in the world is something they don't want to see because it reminds them that they are not living up to their own potential. They don't want to be reminded of that.

Our fear is that it will be "lonely at the top" because others will pull away from us if we are truly successful. The reality however is that it's not lonely at the top. When you are powerfully self-expressed you just hang out with new friends who are also being powerfully self-expressed.

Trying To Force An Outcome

This central Core Dynamic is the result of being conditioned to feel that we are our ego. It happens just by growing up in an environment where everyone feels that they are the collection of their life stories, accomplishments, disappointments, traumas, pleasures and all their other experiences. This modeling seeps into us by osmosis. After all, if everyone is going around believing that they are the collection of their life experiences there isn't really any other frame of reference available from which to learn.

The consequence of this conditioning is that we feel like an isolated individual. We feel separate from and at odds with the universe. This isolation causes us to tend to feel that if something is going to happen then I better make it happen. This is the illusion of being "the doer." It is the illusion of "authorship of action." For those who have the idea that "I create my reality," the very mention of the idea of "the illusion of being the doer" sounds strange. "Of course I'm the doer. I can make my life happen the way that I want it to." This is the powerful voice of this conditioning.

Everyone has had the experience of having a desire, forgetting about it, and then having the desire fulfilled without seeming to have had to take any action at all. This is because in actuality the laws of nature are doing everything even when it seems that our body, mind and personality are involved in the process. It is only our identification with our body, mind, personality, thoughts, actions, etc. that causes us to believe that we are "the doer," that we are an individual.

But when you experience Pure Awareness you find that what you are at your essence isn't your body, your mind, your thoughts, your experiences, your personality, your opinions, etc. You are limitless pure potential to be and experience anything. Think for a moment about the experience referred to as being in the zone. This concept is frequently talked about in relationship to sports. When someone is playing in the zone, time slows down, everything is effortless, it seems almost like you are not doing it (and you're not by the way). It's happening to you and through you rather than you doing it. This is just what happened in those times when you had a desire, didn't do anything yourself to make it happen, and then the result of your desire just effortlessly showed up. That's being in the zone. That's being in sync with the universe.

The universe operates on a law called The Law of Least Action also sometimes called The Law of Least Effort. The planets travel around the sun in a path of least effort, an ellipse, not a square or rectangle. This law of least effort is what is what is operating as plants grow. It's the law that causes electrons to spin around the nucleus of an atom. It governs the rise and fall of the tides and every other natural process. Everything in nature happens with least effort and in perfect timing. This includes everything that happens to us as well. However, our conditioning of thinking and feeling that we are an isolated individual "doer" who is creating our reality, causes us to force and struggle and suffer in trying to "make it happen" MY WAY and IN MY TIMING!

Forcing things to happen your way or in your timing may result in superficially seeming to get what it is that you think you want. It is our identification with our ego that causes us to attempt to coerce life into showing up the way that we want it to. When we think and feel that we are separate from the rest of the universe that we are isolated and alone then we really can't help but try to make things happen the way that we think they should. However, our inability to sense the natural timing of things, our over-riding urge to try to control how things happen causes us to attempt to force outcomes. What is needed is to learn to relax and allow life to show up in its own perfection and natural effortless timing. However this is something that we are deeply conditioned not to do. Thus we struggle and suffer needlessly because we are out of sync with the law of least effort.

Trying To Force An Outcome expresses itself as:

- Excluding Other Perspectives
- Manufacturing Interpretations
- Over-reacting to Circumstances

Excluding Other Perspectives

This expression of Trying To Force An Outcome occurs when we are identified with the way we see the world. This Core Dynamic is where bigotry and prejudice live. It is the source of most disagreement, fighting and wars in the world. It is expressed in all forms of fundamentalism. This is the real basis of religious wars, ethnic and racial discrimination, and much of the inability of people to get along with each other collectively as well as in individual relationships.

When you become identified with your perspective, your particular beliefs become part of your self-definition. They really are not who you are but they compellingly feel like they are really a part of you. This makes you very vulnerable to having your sense of self be threatened if you allow yourself to be open to seeing things in a new or different way. Your way becomes the only way, not only for you but for everyone. "My way or the Highway!" You can't afford to be open to another way of seeing things as it is too much of a threat to your very sense of your existence. So you stay closed minded and isolated, feeling that you are right and how can all these other stupid people in the world not see things like you do. They are heretics and unbelievers. I'm right and they are wrong. I need to be right in order to maintain the sense of my self.

Manufacturing Interpretations

We all know people who have been adversely affected in the past and they can't get over it. The event is long gone but the stories about the event live on in the mind of the person so much so that they are living inside of their story and cannot be fully present. They can also live in a story about how things will be in the future either positive or negative. Whether the story is about the past or the future it absorbs our attention and occupies our mind and it seems like the story is a part of who we are.

Attempting to make meaning of our experiences is a very human thing to do. But when we become identified with the stories that we make up about our experiences and live in these stories as if the events were still impinging upon our life we are then no longer present to the reality of what is. This is an obvious block to living in Pure Awareness all the time. Most people spend so much of their time trying to understand and make sense of their experiences that they rarely live in the present moment. This conditioning is identification with our thinking and intellect. It isn't possible to simply stop being absorbed in our stories just because we understand that we do this and decide not to. The conditioning will dominate your experience and you'll tend to be caught up in the stories until you learn how to experientially extract your awareness from being identified with the story. The Pure Awareness Techniques will teach you how to do this.

Over-reacting to Circumstances

When we become overly identified with our stories we start to expect life to show up the way that we think it should. Our expectations are created out of stories that we make up in our mind that are disconnected from reality. Whenever we are caught up in an expectation we are living in the illusion that the universe will organize life the way that we want it to. When it doesn't we tend to over-react with anger, disappointment or a wide range of other possible emotions. This over-reaction keeps us absorbed inside of the energy of our emotional reaction. We stay identified with the expectation, the story out of which the expectation has been made and to our "legitimate" emotional reaction. As you will see when you learn and experience the SEE Technique, the expectation, story and emotional reaction are all illusions that we get lost to. You will experience how liberating it is to extract yourself from such identifications and experience yourself as your essential nature – Pure Awareness.

Why the Core Dynamics Are Important

The Core Dynamics provide us with penetrating insights into why and how we get lost to the illusions created by our conditioning. You will see as we progress through the book why each Pure Awareness Technique is needed to guide you back from the particular kind of illusion you have become lost to and precisely how to come out of its grip. You are about to embark on a great journey, perhaps one of the most important ones of your life. You are about to learn and experience not only who and what you really are, but also how you can live in an awakened state every moment for the rest of your life.

Each Core Dynamic is a description of a particular way in which you have become lost to an illusion that you are separate from life itself, that you are an isolated individual. By understanding the essence of each of the Core Dynamics you can then see what is needed in order to extract yourself from your conditioning and re-establish the direct experience of wholeness.

So for example, the Core Dynamic of *Resisting Feeling Things Fully* needs a method of being able to do the opposite of this deep-seated conditioning. Instead of staying stuck in the energy of unresolved feelings or emotional reactions caused by unmet expectations you can use the CORE and SEE Techniques.

When you are absorbed in the kind of conditioning that causes you to look outside of yourself for validation, respect, love, attention, etc., in other words when you are caught in the Core Dynamic of Looking for Yourself Where You Are Not, the real need is to look for yourself where you are! You can experience this by using the GAP and AGAPE Techniques to experience that who and what you are is already whole and complete and that you don't need anything from outside of yourself to validate your wholeness.

But it is most important to understand that every type of conditioning is a problem at an experiential level. These are not intellectual problems. They are problems with the way in which you experience life. This is why the Pure Awareness Techniques are all experiential, not intellectual.

Every experience we have in our life has both the circumstance that we find ourselves in, and our reaction to the circumstances. Many times we can't do much, if anything, about the circumstances. But we can learn how to do something about our reactions to those circumstances. When you are caught up in the emotion of your reaction it's very difficult to even see the circumstances clearly, not to mention being able to respond to them in a way that is beneficial to you. With the insights of the Core Dynamics and the liberating effects of the Pure Awareness Techniques you can readily resolve your conditioned reactions and come back to a place of clarity and calm so that you can then make decisions about your life that are really aligned with what is best for you.

There is a synergy between the Core Dynamics and the Pure Awareness Techniques. As the Core Dynamics provide insights into the details of how you become identified with everything that you are not, so do the Pure Awareness Techniques provide the experiential pathways back to the direct experience of what you are. Whether it is simply experiencing your essential nature via the GAP Technique or coming out of the grip of an emotional reaction with the SEE Technique or resolving an incomplete experience with the Core Technique, all of the Pure Awareness Techniques bring you out of your illusions of separateness and back to the direct experience of your essential nature.

When you find that you are unhappy with your life or that you are caught up in problems or reactions, or whatever is going on with you, the Core Dynamics can always provide a distinction between what is happening and your reactions to what is happening. Whenever you are stuck in life take a look at the Core Dynamics Model and see which of the 12 Core Dynamics is being expressed. It can be just one of the dynamics or several of the dynamics at play. Then use the appropriate Pure Awareness Technique to bring yourself back to the experience of your essential nature. An explanation of the essence of each Core Dynamic and which Pure Awareness Techniques to use to come out of the grip of the Dynamics is in an Appendix at the end of the book.

The Absence of the Core Dynamics of Human Conditioning

As you practice the Pure Awareness Techniques that you learn from this book, you will be dismantling the limitations of your preverbal childhood conditioning in ways that are incredibly effective. You will begin to come out of the grip of your conditioning. You will begin to live a whole new kind of life, a life that is free of the invisible binding influences of the Core Dynamics. When the Core Dynamics are thoroughly absent you live with the lively presence of Pure Awareness all the time. Here's what life is like when the Core Dynamics are gone.

The Levels of Life

Another useful model that is a part of Human Software Engineering is called The Levels of Life. This is a simple model that is helpful for assessing at what level a problem truly originates. Here's what it looks like:

The Levels of Life

Bio-mechanical

Bio-chemical

Bio-energetic

Bio-awareness

The basic premise is that matter (the Bio-mechanical level) is made up of molecules (the Bio-chemical level). As mentioned before, molecules are made up of atoms and sub-atomic particles. Molecules, atoms and sub-atomic particles have electro-magnetic fields and are, according to physics, ultimately made up of waves of energy (the Bio-energetic level). We can also think of everything that exists as coming into being out of some intention, either human or otherwise (the Bio-awareness level). We certainly know from physics that just having an observer present changes the experiment. So it is apparent that awareness impacts energy. Some philosophers and ancient texts such as the Vedas assert that everything is made up of vibrating consciousness. Accordingly Pure Awareness, Pure Consciousness is the source of all of these levels and they arise in this hierarchical structure. Pure Awareness transcends and is at the basis of all of the levels of life and the Bio-awareness level is its first level of expression or manifestation.

The Bio-mechanical level includes things that you see and touch with your senses. It involves mechanical forms of debugging and upgrading your life like setting broken bones, having dental work, or a massage or simply washing your hands. These are all mechanical in nature.

The Bio-chemical level of course involves things like diet, medicines, herbs, drugs, nutritional supplements, etc.

The Bio-energetic level includes such things as cell phone and other wireless signals, homeopathic remedies, Bach Flower Remedies, ultra-sound, radiation, CAT Scans, X-rays, brainwaves, the WaveMakerä and the ultra-weak electrical signals and electromagnetic fields within the body.

The Bio-awareness level of life includes thoughts, feelings, intentions, conditioned responses, intuitions, judgments, ideas, affirmations, desires, premonitions, projections, identifications emotional reactions and the emotional pain stored in our bodies.

Most people have been trained to see the world primarily from a Bio-mechanical and Bio-chemical mind set. However, if a problem originates as a deep inner conflict at the level of Bio-awareness then it is unlikely that cutting it out or taking a drug to mask its presence will be the optimal solution. In fact if the problem originates at a deeper level then you won't really resolve it unless you approach it at the appropriate level.

For example, a recent scientific study called the ACE Study (Adverse Childhood Experience Study), done at Kaiser Permanente in San Diego, California with over 17,000 participants found that there are clear graded correlations between the extent of unresolved childhood traumas (Bio-awareness level) and a wide range of physical illnesses (Bio-chemical and Bio-mechanical levels) found in participants lives half a century after the original traumas occurred. It is clear from the ACE Study that the unresolved traumas are significant contributors to health problems later in life. Conventional medicine, based mainly on the Bio-mechanical and Bio-chemical levels of life is at a loss for what to do about the unresolved childhood traumas because doctors are not trained in effective Bio-awareness level techniques. The level of investment in the development of new drugs, medical equipment and surgical techniques is staggering. Yet all of this investment is pretty much useless if a problem really originates at a deeper level. All that can be done is to suppress symptoms which is not a very satisfactory solution.

Although Human Software Engineering encompasses all four levels of life, it is primarily concerned with the Bio-energetic and Bio-awareness levels. Thus the focus of inquiry and development of technologies and techniques is designed to get at the real level where the "bugs" truly are in our systems.

The Core Dynamics of Human Conditioning insights provide the roadmap of the nature of one major and important category of these bugs. It is a roadmap of the Bio-awareness level of problems caused by our pre-verbal conditioning.

The Pure Awareness Techniques provide a new technology of consciousness for dealing with so many problems that are rooted in us at the Bio-awareness level of life.

Yet another set of technologies, the WaveMaker and WaveMaker Pro are devices designed for debugging and upgrading work at the Bio-energetic level of life. These devices use the principle of wave interference from physics to weaken or cancel out unwanted energy patterns in the body (debugging) or strengthen and stabilize the natural electro-magnetic fields within the body (Upgrade). For more information and links to web pages about these HSE devices see the section on Internet Resources near the end of the book.

In The Power of How, the aspects of Human Software Engineering that we are exploring are those that reside at the Bio-awareness level. It is the Bio-awareness level at which the Core Dynamics provide penetrating insights into the nature of the "bugs" in our inner human software and the Pure Awareness Techniques help us debug ourselves to remove the inner barriers to living from Pure Awareness all the time.

What is Pure Awareness?

Pure Awareness is very simple. It is that attribute of you that is your awakeness, your aliveness. It is the screen of your mind upon which fall all of your thoughts and perceptions. It is your consciousness. It is that with which you experience everything.

Pure Awareness is so simple that we don't notice that it is there. Because Pure Awareness is not an object of experience itself and is only in the background for our experiences we don't normally notice that it is there. It's too simple, too silent, too... uninteresting!

Although most people are completely unaware that they have something called Pure Awareness within them it is absolutely the most important part of us. In fact it is our essential nature. It is our very aliveness. It is what gives us the ability to perceive and think and experience life.

Throughout recorded history, the experience of Pure Awareness has been a spiritual quest for untold thousands of seekers of truth. Meditation and other spiritual practices aspire to attain the direct experience of Pure Awareness. Pure Awareness goes by many names; Samadhi, Satori, Transcendental Consciousness, the Source, the Now, the Presence, the Absolute, Universality, Wholeness, and Enlightenment! The transcendentalists Ralph Waldo Emerson, Henry David Thoreau, Margaret Fuller and others attempted to describe it in their writings. Some authors on the subject describe having an experience of Pure Awareness only to lose it and then struggle for years trying to recapture the experience again.

In the spiritual traditions of the world people dedicate countless hours, days, years and even lifetimes in the pursuit of the experience of Pure Awareness. There are many disparate notions and a myriad of diverse practices, some of which are quite austere, that people have pursued for many years in the faint hope of catching a glimpse of Pure Awareness. And yet, as you will soon see, all that is needed is to look in the right place and you can experience Pure Awareness. It is so incredibly simple! Anyone can do this and have the experience of Pure Awareness in a moment. It's really that easy.

chapter 4

Overview of the Eight Pure Awareness Techniques

Section One – How to Experience Pure Awareness

GAP

We start with the simplest way of experiencing Pure Awareness by using a technique called the GAP – an acronym for Greater Awareness Place. This is done by simply directing your awareness to notice itself as the silent background in which your thoughts occur. I'll give you clear simple guidelines for exactly how to do this in the full description of the GAP Technique in the detailed section about the GAP Technique a little further into the book.

> *GAP – an acronym for Greater Awareness Place. This is done by simply directing your awareness to notice itself as the silent background in which your thoughts occur. I'll give you clear simple guidelines for exactly how to do this in the full description of the GAP Technique in the detailed section about the GAP Technique a little further into the book.*

AGAPE

Once you learn how to experience Pure Awareness as the background of silence in which your thoughts occur, you can then learn to experience Pure Awareness as permeating the entire universe by using AGAPE – an acronym for Accessing Greater Awareness Place Everywhere. This is not just an idea that Pure Awareness permeates the entire universe, as lots of people have written about, but rather a direct experience of Pure Awareness filling the entire universe. Practicing the AGAPE Technique will also give you the experience of your essential nature – Pure Awareness – as the essential nature of every other person and every other thing that you can ever experience.

Section 2 – How to Debug Your Ego

Debug the Identifications that Create Your Ego

The ego exists because of your identifications with the stories that comprise it. Unless you are able to experience Pure Awareness as your essential nature, you believe whole-heartedly that the ego is who you are. The way to debug the ego is to debug your identification with the stories, expectations, projections and reactions that make it up. How to do this is to directly experience Pure Awareness as the silent background in which your thoughts, feelings and perceptions occur. But what if you can't experience the silent background in which your thoughts occur?

Typically, when it is difficult to experience the silence it is because you may be so caught in the grip of an emotional reaction that you become lost it. It's as if you become that emotion. There seems to be no silence when you're gripped by emotions. The grip feels so powerful that there just doesn't seem to be any silence inside of you at all. You expect things to turn out a certain way but they don't and now you are upset. Expectations are part of the Core Dynamic – Over-reacting to Circumstances. When you act from this dynamic you'll likely say, "What background of silence? What are you talking about?"

SEE

When you are caught up in the grip of an emotional reaction to an unmet expectation you won't feel like you have access to that silent background in which the thoughts occur. You are having a reaction and it isn't pretty. This will also be your experience if you are caught up in the emotion of fear caused by projecting a possible negative outcome onto the future. The technique for extracting yourself from being lost to such emotions is the SEE Technique - an acronym for Side Entrance Expansion. It's a technique for very quickly and directly experiencing the distinction between being lost to your emotion and then being in Pure Awareness. The SEE Technique allows you to so easily and quickly come out of the grip of an emotional reaction that it will amaze you. When you are out of the grip of the emotion and in the direct experience of Pure Awareness you will recognize that your reaction was based on a story that you had made up, a story that wasn't even real. It was and expectation that life would happen in a particular way or you were projecting something on to the future that only existed in your mind.

WONDER

Next is the WONDER Technique – an acronym for Wait On Neutral During Emotional Reactions. You can also think of this as "Unplugging the Power Cord" or "Shifting To Neutral" because that is exactly what we do when using the WONDER Technique. The WONDER technique helps you to stop engaging in ego-driven habits that tend to perpetuate themselves without you seeming to have any control over them. These are the habits that keep you stuck in ways of being that simply no longer work for you. They comprise the part of the ego that is made up of your habitual ways of being. We are often so identified with our habits that we engage in them as if they were actually a part of who we are. They aren't. It just feels like they are. By using the WONDER Technique you will learn how to nip them in the bud and let them sink back into nothingness. This process creates a gap of awareness that frees you from identification with the habit. With just a little practice the unconscious cluelessness of habits vaporizes. You won't have to replace the old habit with a new one, because you will be making choices and taking action from the "wonder" of uncertainty - responding spontaneously to the needs of the moment with the fullness of your being.

Section 3 – How to Know that You Know

Another attribute of genuine spiritual experience is that you know from deep within yourself and you don't need to justify this kind of knowing with your intellect. This concept may seem quite foreign to most people as we are so deeply conditioned to rely on our mind and intellect as a way of "knowing." But using your intellect may not be the best tool to use for important decisions like who to marry, what career to choose, and where to live, etc. You are making decisions constantly. Wouldn't it be ideal to have your decisions be truly aligned with what is really optimal for you and your life? In fact, wouldn't it be great to be able to rely on your inner knowing for everything in your life. When you are living in Pure Awareness all the time you only make decisions from this inner place of knowing.

SANYAMA

We can cultivate the ability to access our inner knowing and begin to get the clear distinction between our knowing and our conditioned thinking by using a Pure Awareness Technique called SANYAMA. SANYAMA is originally a word from the Sanskrit language that was used to describe a technique of dropping a desire or question into Pure Awareness and getting a response. Yogi Patanjali who is thought by some to be the father of the whole field of yoga originally described this practice in his "Yoga Sutras."

I discovered that the word SANYAMA could also be used as an acronym that beautifully describes the process – Silent Awareness Notices Your Answers Manifesting Automatically. In the process of learning SANYAMA you will also learn how to access and use your "subtle senses." What are the subtle senses? Consider it in this way – assuming that you are reading this book silently you are probably hearing the words in your mind as you read them. The question is, "Are you hearing these words with your ears?" Obviously not! Just the fact that we hear thoughts in our awareness and not with our ears is a pretty clear indication that our senses are not completely dependent upon our sensory organs. Having images in the mind's eye is another example. We don't see these visualizations with our eyes but rather with our "mind's eye." We see them in our consciousness.

Practicing the SANYAMA Technique cultivates familiarity with using your subtle senses. This technique develops the ability to clearly distinguish between your thinking and your knowing. As you get good at it you begin to have clearer and clearer perception of your knowing. Your perception using your subtle senses will begin to extend outwards in both time and space. One outgrowth of this is that you begin to trust and act on your intuition more and more. You will also develop the ability to "remember the future"- to know things before they happen. These capabilities are natural aspects of a state of spiritual enlightenment and can be easily cultivated though practicing the SANYAMA Technique.

WAIT

An additional technique to cultivate your inner knowing is to learn to WAIT. WAIT is an acronym for Waiting Accesses Intuitive Truth. WAIT is a technique for bringing yourself into alignment with the law of least effort. Have you ever had a desire and then forgotten about it for a time and then all of a sudden the fulfillment of your desire just showed up without you doing anything to bring it about? The WAIT Technique helps you to live like that all the time.

When you learn how to wait for the perfect timing for things, they happen, either seemly by themselves, or with an "in the zone" like effortlessness.

Section 4 – How to Debug the Emotional Pain of the Past

When we are little we are easily emotionally overwhelmed. We have a delicate nervous system that doesn't yet have the capacity to process many of the intense emotional experiences that we have as a very young child. As a result we end up not completing many of our intense emotional experiences and it appears that these become stored in our body. These incomplete experiences become our "emotional baggage." Everyone seems to have plenty of these and they produce a kind of screen or barrier to our natural experience of Pure Awareness.

CORE

What is needed is an efficient way to complete these incomplete overwhelming emotional experiences from the past. The CORE Technique – an acronym for Center of Remaining Energy is the most efficient way I have found for doing this. It is a process of doing the opposite of what you are deeply conditioned to do. You are conditioned to go away from the intensity of the energy of emotional pain stored in the body. When using the CORE Technique you dive right into the center of the most intense part of the energy of the incomplete emotional experience that is held in your body.

Allowing yourself to feel into the most intense part of the energy of an incomplete experience of emotional intensity is VERY different than simply "feeling your feelings." It is as different as a flash of light beam is from a laser beam. Laser beams can be so powerful that they can cut through very hard materials. A flashlight can penetrate the darkness but can't cut through anything else.

Similarly the process of just feeling the energy of a feeling is inefficient for completing incomplete intense emotional experiences. The CORE Technique is a laser like way to feel into and complete emotional energy. It penetrates down into the heart of the most intense part of the energy of the incomplete experience. This allows you to rapidly and thoroughly complete the experience of the energy that is held there. When the energy is complete your awareness naturally returns to the inner experience of wholeness. Using the Core Technique helps to debug incomplete unresolved emotional energy that keeps you from living in Pure Awareness all the time.

Imagine for a moment that the suitcases filled with incomplete emotional pain from the past are like a layer of cheese between you and Pure Awareness. Each time you use the CORE Technique to complete one of your incomplete intense emotional experiences you make a hole in the cheese. The cheese becomes more like Swiss cheese. The idea is to keep making holes in the Swiss cheese until there is little to no cheese blocking Pure Awareness from shining through unobstructed.

GPS

When there are subtler residual patterns of emotional energy held in the body that are difficult to get access too there is a simple way to bring them into awareness. This technique is called the GPS Technique – an acronym for Gentle Provocation System. The GPS Technique is used as a kind of vacuum cleaner for cleaning up any residual emotional energy of incomplete experiences when it is otherwise not easy to determine if something is still held in your system or not. It is a combined use of the SANYAMA Technique and the CORE Technique.

Now that you have an overview of what gets in the way of living in Pure Awareness all the time and the Pure Awareness Techniques to change this, it is time to go in depth into exactly HOW to practice the Pure Awareness Techniques so that you can apply and integrate them into your life.

chapter 5

The Pure Awareness Techniques

Section One – How to Experience Pure Awareness

How to Experience Pure Awareness Right Now

The GAP Technique — Greater Awareness Place

"It's so simple! When Tom guided our class through the GAP exercise I thought it was going to be something that might be difficult to do. But to my surprise and delight I was easily able to do it the first time. You just look off to the side of your thoughts and there it is, your own Awareness. And people have been trying so hard to find themselves, all the while there you are, right there just off to the side of your thoughts. You just have to know where to look. Amazing!

– Patricia Coleman

In order for this book to make sense to you it is necessary for you to experience Pure Awareness directly before we go too far. You may already be familiar with the experience of Pure Awareness but whether you are or not, I highly recommend that you do one of two things:

One, listen to an audio recording of my guiding someone through the experience of the GAP Technique located on the web page – www. thepowerofhow.com/GAP.html

Type this URL into your web browser and when you access the page you can listen to the recording in which I guide you to experience Pure Awareness within yourself. This is quite easy, and will only take a few minutes.

Two, if you have no access to the web then have someone read to you the steps to experiencing the GAP Technique from the script that follows shortly. Because the GAP Technique is best done with your eyes closed it is much easier to have someone read the steps to you rather than trying to do it yourself.

How to do the GAP Technique

Experiencing the Background of Silence in Which Your
Thoughts Occur

The purpose of this exercise is to experience the background of silence in which your thoughts occur, to shift your attention from an outward direction to an inward direction so that it is possible to experience the essential nature of awareness itself. Recent scientific research in neuroscience confirms that there are periods of inactivity in the brain that correspond to the gaps between thoughts.

To start this technique you'll want to sit quietly and close your eyes. Wait for about half a minute so that you can simply experience what it is like to sit with your eyes closed. Then have your reader say the following:

"Notice that with your eyes closed you experience several kinds of things. You hear my voice, you may notice the feeling

of your body sitting in the chair, you may notice other noises or sensations, and you will notice that there are thoughts coming to you."

"Notice that thoughts occur in a similar way to how we speak; they don't come in one long run-on sentence. There are pauses or gaps, however brief, in between the thoughts."

"Allow yourself to simply notice the gap in between the thoughts."

Now wait for about half a minute

"Notice that the gaps between thoughts are truly empty. There is nothing there. The nothingness is just Pure Awareness without the awareness of anything else. It is lively but there is no object of experience."

"Another way to directly experience this nothingness of Pure Awareness is to simply notice that there is a silence that is in the background of your thoughts. Some people find it easier to just shift their attention from noticing the activity of the thoughts to noticing the silent background in which the thoughts are occurring."

"As you notice the silent background in which the thoughts are occurring, you will notice that you can be aware of the silence even while the thoughts are coming and going. Allow yourself to simply favor noticing that silent background. Immerse yourself in that silence."

Wait about one minute

"If you find that you have become absorbed in thinking, at the moment when you notice this, simply bring your attention back

to the gap between the thoughts or the background of silence."

Wait one to two minutes

Then say

"Okay. When you're ready, open your eyes."

_____

So now that you have tried the GAP Technique - what did you experience? What was it like? What are the attributes of Pure Awareness?

You probably experienced it as quiet, peaceful and expansive. It's pleasant, relaxing. It's very uhmm... nice.

From here on, when I use the term Pure Awareness, you'll now know from your experience what I'm talking about. You now know what Pure Awareness is. It is just the silent background in which your thoughts occur. It is the silent awareness with which you are experiencing your thoughts, even the thoughts of the words you are reading now.

Now that you have had your own experience of Pure Awareness, you might notice that Pure Awareness is always there, lively in the background, even with your eyes open and with the activity of thoughts and perceptions occurring. Can you still feel the presence of the Pure Awareness? If not, you can easily bring yourself back to it by simply doing the GAP Technique again. But once you have experienced it you may very well be able to simply notice that the silent background is there even as you are reading these words.

Was there anything lacking in the experience of Pure Awareness? Was there anything that you could not do from this place? Was there any sense of feeling needy while you are in the experience of Pure Awareness? When you have a true experience of Pure Awareness the answers to these questions are "No." This is because you cannot find the things or perceptions of your ego in Pure Awareness.

If you aren't sure whether you had a clear experience of Pure Awareness or not, this is to be expected. After all, remember that every experience that you have ever had is an experience of some THING or some object of perception. Pure Awareness is actually so simple because there is no-thing there. Our lives are so focused in an outward direction that we tend to not know or remember that this silent Pure Awareness is the essence of what we are.

Pure Awareness seems therefore very abstract and so unlike all of our other experiences that it is common when you first experience it to not be sure that you did. After all, if you have not experienced Pure Awareness before, your only database of experiences prior to a few moments ago was of the experience of THINGS. So if you aren't sure if you experienced Pure Awareness go back and go through the exercise again. Remember that you are not trying to experience something that's an object. Pure Awareness is just the silent witness of your experiences. It is just awareness itself. It is the "you" that is experiencing everything. This is why it can be called your essential nature.

Now that you practiced the GAP Technique you can see what I mean by how simple and easy it is to experience Pure Awareness. This is because there is nowhere to go and nothing to do. It is just a matter of noticing the background of silence in which your thoughts and perceptions are occurring. That's it. It is simply your own awareness being aware of itself!

The experience of Pure Awareness is unique because all of our other experiences are characterized by perceiving objects of experience, like this book and the words printed on the pages, the feeling of the paper and binding that you are touching with your hands, the sounds that the pages make as you turn them, the taste of the food that you had at your last meal or snack.

Remember, as I mentioned previously, all of the sensory experiences that we have are comprised of three components: The experiencer, the process of experiencing and the object of experience.

But the experience of Pure Awareness that you just had is different. It is your awareness being aware of Awareness itself. That means Awareness is Aware of Awareness. Awareness is not an object of experience. There is no perceiving going on. There is just a state of being purely aware. This is why we call it Pure Awareness because it isn't anything but Awareness experiencing itself.

Once you have done the GAP exercise and experienced Pure Awareness you now have the experiential basis for understanding the rest of this book. Congratulations! You've already learned one of the Pure Awareness Techniques!

Anytime you want to refresh your experience of Pure Awareness, take a few minutes and experience it again. Here's the URL for the recording as a reminder. **www.thepowerofhow.com/GAP.html**

More About Doing the GAP Technique

Now that you know how to do the GAP Technique there are some subtleties that may be helpful to understand. First you have probably noticed that there are two ways to become aware of Pure Awareness during the GAP Technique. One is bringing your awareness to the silence between thoughts and the other is bringing your awareness to the silent background in which your thoughts occur. Both of them are more easily done with your eyes closed. In both cases it is good to start off the exercise by allowing yourself to become aware of thoughts occurring in your mind.

Sometimes you simply can't notice that there are gaps or pauses in between the thoughts because there seem to be too many thoughts racing through your mind. This can happen when you are emotionally upset or disturbed about something. In this case you need to shift to using the SEE Technique to access Pure Awareness out beyond the outer edge of the energy of the emotion you are experiencing, or the CORE Technique to complete the incomplete experience that is currently dominating your inner experience (you will learn how to do these techniques in the coming chapters). Once you resolve the emotional energy then you will have a more settled state of being and you will be able to notice the background of silence by experiencing it in the gaps in between your thoughts or by just looking off to the side of the thoughts and noticing the silent background.

Similarly, the background of silence in which our thoughts occur is often overshadowed by the "loudness" of our thoughts. Our thoughts are active, have meaning, and can be colored with emotion. They are certainly more engaging when it comes to content than the background of silence in which they are occurring. Thoughts tend to attract our attention more than the silence does.

Normally we don't pay any attention to the background of silence. Just as we don't pay attention to the silence in our living room when music is playing; or when we go to the movies we become absorbed in the images that are falling on the screen. We don't pay attention to the blank white screen that allows the images to be seen. The images dominate our experience.

To experience your essential nature which is your own Pure Awareness, it is a matter of simply "looking off to the side" of the thoughts and noticing that the thoughts are occurring in a background of silence. The beauty of "looking off to the side of your thoughts" to experience Pure Awareness is that it can be done even when the mind is racing with lots of thoughts. This may be why some people prefer noticing the background of silence approach over noticing the gaps between thoughts. Use which ever method you are comfortable with. Either one will give you access to the experience of Pure Awareness.

Thoughts, Thoughts and More Thoughts—What Do I Do?

Sometimes people are concerned that they will get absorbed in thinking and that this gets in the way of the experience of Pure Awareness. Having an understanding about the role of thoughts during the GAP Technique and knowing how to handle them is important.

The real secret is that there is nothing to handle. Having thoughts occur is not a barrier to experiencing Pure Awareness. It is perfectly possible to experience Pure Awareness and have thoughts occurring at the same time. It is a matter of what you favor noticing with your attention. People are deeply habituated to noticing their thoughts. I would go so far as to say that just about everyone seems to be addicted to thinking. It is often used as a "drug of choice" to avoid feeling things.

This doesn't mean that having thoughts is a barrier to experiencing the background of silence. It is perfectly possible to experience Pure Awareness even while thoughts are occurring. It's a bit like being able to see the sky on a partly cloudy day. As long as the clouds aren't completely covering the sky we can see some sky. Just as it is possible to shift your attention from noticing the clouds to noticing the sky in the background, it is also possible to shift your attention from noticing your thoughts to noticing the background of silence in which your thoughts are occurring. Just as you can read a book with birds chirping outside or with the hum of traffic on a nearby freeway, in general you have the ability to direct your attention to favor noticing one thing more than something else. It's just that we are so deeply conditioned to only notice our thoughts that we don't even know that there is a silent background in which the thoughts occur - until now.

As you do the GAP Technique, notice how easily accessible the background of silence in which the thoughts are occurring is. This silence is your own Pure Awareness. It is your consciousness. It is that aspect of you that allows you to experience all of life. This is why we refer to it as your essential nature. It is the silent witness or the observer of your experiences.

As you practice noticing Pure Awareness in the background of silence in which your thoughts occur, you may have very clear extended experiences of Pure Awareness where there doesn't seem to be any thoughts at all. The thoughts fade so much into the background that you hardly notice them. This is a very deep and satisfying experience. You may notice feeling refreshed and fully alive, while at the same time feeling deeply rested and relaxed.

As you practice the GAP Technique for longer periods of time, say 10 to 20 minutes, you may also have the simultaneous experience of becoming absorbed in thinking for what seem to be long periods of many minutes. Sometimes when this happens people think that they are doing the GAP Technique incorrectly or that they are not experiencing Pure Awareness. Nothing could be further from the truth.

When you become lost to thoughts during the GAP Technique it is actually because the technique is working beautifully! Here is why -

When we shift our attention to noticing the background of silence in which the thoughts are occurring our mind settles down. This is because it is less active. As our mind settles down it is natural for the body to settle down as well. This causes us to feel deeply relaxed.

Our bodies want to be free of stress and strain. When we go into Pure Awareness and the body begins to correspondingly relax it is natural for the body to begin to release any stresses or strains that may have accumulated.

Such releases naturally create subtle activity in the body. This is because the presence of the stress in the body causes a kind of physical tension where the stress is held. When we begin to experience the deeper relaxed, rested state during the GAP Technique, these physical knots of stress begin to unwind themselves. This creates movement and activity in our mind because the mind and body are so intimately connected. When you practice the GAP Technique and you become absorbed in thoughts, it is actually a very positive by-product of the phenomenon of releasing stress.

For that matter, people have also reported sometimes falling asleep during the GAP Technique. When you take the mind into Pure Awareness the body takes whatever it needs. When someone falls asleep during the GAP Technique it is caused by the body releasing some accumulated fatigue. It's all quite natural. When you practice the GAP Technique, if your body needs to release stress or fatigue, it will take the opportunity to give itself what it needs. This is just the simple process of release of stress causing the activity of thinking or the release of fatigue causing sleep.

Therefore, if you have lots of thoughts during a particular session of the GAP Technique, it actually means that you have successfully accessed the GAP and settled the mind down even if it only took a very short time to produce the rested state that allowed the thoughts to begin to come. Becoming absorbed in thoughts during the GAP Technique only means that the body is releasing some stresses and strains. This in turn is creating the activity of thinking and your mind becomes quite occupied with this activity. This is experienced as thoughts in the mind. It's not from doing it wrong. On the contrary, it is from doing the technique correctly!

So don't have the attitude that thoughts shouldn't be there. It's natural for them to be there. It is also natural for you to shift from noticing Pure Awareness to noticing the thoughts. Here's what you do about it.

When you notice that you have been absorbed in thinking, don't bother to chastise yourself. Actually, something good has just happened—you've released some stress. When the body has released enough stress that you become aware that you've been thinking, now it is time to go back into the GAP and experience Pure Awareness again.

Simply allow for the naturalness of both thinking and noticing Pure Awareness in the background of silence. There is a natural shifting back and forth between noticing Pure Awareness and being absorbed in thinking. The idea is to become familiar with Pure Awareness by using the GAP Technique. Eventually you never lose the experience of Pure Awareness and it isn't overshadowed by thoughts or anything else. When you develop this state of being you experience Pure Awareness as present all the time, 24/7, 365—it never goes away. That's what we're after. When you reach this state (which can develop quite quickly with regularly using the Pure Awareness Techniques) not only will you be able to maintain the experience of Pure Awareness while you are having thoughts but even while having intense experiences of pleasure or pain. In this state you are never lost to your experiences and you experience a shift of the sense of who you are from being an individual to being Pure Awareness, which is the true reality of what you really are.

When to Use the GAP Technique

- As a regular daily practice to become very familiar with the experience of Pure Awareness.

- Before doing something important and you would like to be operating from wholeness.

- While working with a Core Dynamics Coach to experience that you are already whole and complete.

- Any time you want to directly experience Pure Awareness.

You can use the GAP Technique whenever you like, whenever you want to experience Pure Awareness. Some people make a regular practice of the GAP Technique and use it as a form of meditation that they do once or twice per day, typically in the morning and evening. The more you practice it the more you will cultivate an ever-increasing presence of Pure Awareness. You can find the frequency and duration that suits your individual tastes and desires for developing your awareness of Pure Awareness. Making it a regular practice is highly recommended.

However, you don't want to overdo it either. Sitting around doing the GAP Technique for hours at a time may not be the best plan for integrating the state of Pure Awareness into your life. What is optimal is to toggle back and forth between becoming familiar with Pure Awareness by doing the GAP Technique for short periods and then engaging in your daily activities. Balance is the key. Introducing the GAP Technique into your daily routine starts you on a path of integrating Pure Awareness into your life experience. The value of doing this is enormous.

The GAP Technique is also very useful during Core Dynamics Coaching sessions whenever someone has become overly identified with things in their life. People tend to become identified and attached to their possessions, the people and relationships in their life, their thoughts and ideas, their emotions, reactions, stories and self-definitions. It is in the nature of human conditioning to become identified with both our inner and outer experiences and lose the sense of connection to our own essential nature—Pure Awareness.

During Core Dynamics Coaching sessions the Core Dynamics Coach will use the GAP Technique to gently guide their client back to the experience of Pure Awareness when he/she identifies that the person needs to experience the inner reference of who they really are. The GAP is a great experiential antidote when people have slipped into getting the sense of who they are from anything other than Pure Awareness. This quickly re-establishes the inner sense of being grounded in one's Self. Many forms of attachment, struggle and suffering just melt away and they are easily recognized for the illusions that they are. The GAP Technique is a simple and fast way to bring someone out of the conditioning of the Core Dynamics categories called Looking for Yourself Where You Are Not and Trying to Force an Outcome.

For more information about Core Dynamics Coaching go to www. thepowerofhow.com on the Internet or

For information about Core Dynamics Coach Training programs go to

www.greatlifetechnologies.com/CDCTraining/Options.html

Remembering to Use the GAP Technique

Remembering to use the GAP Technique is again dependent upon your decision and desire. If you find the experience of the GAP useful and you like the lingering presence of Pure Awareness that develops as you do it more and more, then you may be inspired to practice the GAP Technique on a regular basis or as it suits you. Some people work well with routines and others don't, but it always comes back to a decision. If you decide to use this technique to cultivate your familiarity with Pure Awareness then you will find the perfect frequency and duration that suits your personal situation.

How Using the GAP Technique Impacts Your Life

As you will notice, practicing the GAP Technique can give you a profound sense of inner peace, centeredness, relaxation and expanded awareness. It can rapidly bring you a clear, direct experience of Pure Awareness. This tends to bring about a gradually, increasing familiarity with Pure Awareness and more and more of a sense of awareness and presence in your daily life.

It can also shift how you get the sense of who you are - from thinking of yourself as an isolated individual to experiencing yourself as the totality of Pure Awareness. It is therefore an extremely useful technique.

How to Experience Pure Awareness Everywhere in the Universe

The AGAPE Technique - Accessing Greater Awareness Place Everywhere

"I have practiced many forms of meditation and have had many wonderful experiences. But the first time that Tom took us through the AGAPE Technique it was the most profound experience of expanded consciousness that I had ever had. I didn't want to come back! And as I have used The AGAPE Technique more and more I have developed this profound sense of oneness with everything and everyone. I am so grateful to know how to do this."

– Susan Wight

The AGAPE Pure Awareness Technique starts out with the GAP Technique and gives you the direct experience of Pure Awareness. But it then goes further to give you the experience that Pure Awareness permeates everything in the entire universe. This is not just an idea, or a mere intellectual concept. The AGAPE Technique actually takes you through the direct experience of this.

How to Do the AGAPE Technique

It starts with the GAP Technique and then expands the experience of Pure Awareness from the sense of being localized in your head to your whole body, then to the room you are in, then the house or building that you are in, then the town or city, the country, the world, the solar system, the galaxy, the clusters of galaxies and the entire universe and beyond.

When you open your eyes after having this expansive experience of Pure Awareness, you then allow yourself to feel the presence of Pure Awareness in an object that you can see and then in another person if you are in a place where there is someone else present. You can also imagine someone you know if no one is present in the room.

The result is a sense of expansion of the experience of Pure Awareness that gives you the very real sense of your oneness with the entire universe and everything in it. It gives you the direct experience that what you are at your essence is the essence of every single thing that you could ever experience.

You can access the audio recording that guides you through the experience here—

www.thepowerofhow.com/AGAPE.html

If you don't have access to the Internet you can have a friend read the following instructions to you.

Experience Pure Awareness Everywhere

To start this technique, sit quietly and close your eyes and become aware of the gap between the thoughts or the silent background in which the thoughts occur. Have your reader wait for about half a minute for you to renew your experience of Pure Awareness in the gap. Then have your reader say the following:

"Sometimes when doing the GAP Technique you may have the sense that Pure Awareness seems like it is inside of your head. Notice that, if you allow yourself to, you can feel the lively presence of that Pure Awareness throughout your entire body."

Wait for about half a minute to allow them to experience this

"Notice that, if you allow yourself to, you can feel the lively presence of that same Pure Awareness filling up the room that you are in now. It's already there. You are just allowing yourself to notice that it is there."

Wait about half a minute to allow them to experience this

"If you allow yourself to, you can experience the lively presence of that Pure Awareness permeating the whole building,

Pause for about 10 seconds

and it is permeating the whole city of _____ (name of city where they are)."

Pause for another 10 seconds

"If you allow yourself to, you can feel the lively presence of that same Pure Awareness filling up the entire State of _____ (use the name of the state where they are)."

Wait another 10 seconds

"It's there filling up the _____ (use the name of the country where you are)."

Wait another 10 seconds

"It's there throughout the entire world."

Wait another 10 seconds

"The solar system,"

Wait about 5 seconds

"The galaxy,"

Wait about 5 seconds

"The clusters of galaxies,"

Wait about 5 seconds

"The whole unbounded universe."

Wait about 20 seconds

"Now bring your awareness back to your body. Notice that you can bring your awareness back into your body without losing the sense of that expanded Pure Awareness that's permeating everything in the universe."

Wait about 10 seconds

"Now open your eyes. When you are ready look at an object in the room. Notice that the same lively Pure Awareness is present there. In fact, it is present everywhere."

Wait about 20 seconds

"Now look at a person in the room (or imagine someone you know) and simply notice that the same lively Pure Awareness is there permeating that person. It's the same Pure Awareness that you experience inside of you when you notice the background of silence in which the thoughts occur."

Wait about 20 seconds

"Notice that Pure Awareness is permeating everything. It is the essential nature of what you are, it is the essential nature of what I am and it is the essential nature of everything that exists. That's all there is. It is all vibrating Pure Awareness. Practicing this exercise will help you to cultivate the awareness of Pure Awareness present in everything and will give you an experiential connection to everything and everyone."

This completes the instructions for the AGAPE Technique.

When to Use AGAPE

- Directly following doing the GAP Technique.

- As a regular daily practice to directly experience that the essential nature of who and what you really are - is everywhere in the universe.

- Before doing something that is important to you where you would like to be operating from wholeness and experiencing yourself as being "at one" with everything and everyone such as before a meeting, a presentation, a client session, an exam, or anything where you want to experience your oneness with someone or a group.

- Anytime that you want to experience being one with everything and everyone.

Remembering to Use the AGAPE Technique

The guidelines for remembering to use it are fundamentally the same as for the GAP Technique. Remembering to use the AGAPE Technique is again dependent upon your decision and desire. If you enjoy the heightened and expanded presence of Pure Awareness that the experience of the AGAPE Technique brings you, then you may be inspired to practice it on a regular basis. Because it is a natural extension of the GAP Technique you can go from the GAP right into the AGAPE. If you decide to use this technique to cultivate your increasing familiarity with Pure Awareness then you will find the optimal schedule that suits your situation.

How Using the AGAPE Technique Impacts Your Life

Often people feel isolated and alone, separate and disconnected from others and from life. The AGAPE Technique has a profound effect on bringing you out of the illusion of separateness and giving you a deep sense of connectedness with people, nature, the world and life as a whole.

Section Two – How to Debug Your Ego

How to Debug Your Identifications—the Building Blocks of the Ego

What is the ego? It is the false sense of who we are that we make up in our mind. Indeed it is quite human to be so identified with the stories about our life made up in our mind. We come to believe that this collection of things that we have experienced defines who we are. After all what other reference for *sense of self* do we have? In the absence of the direct experience of your essential nature, Pure Awareness, it is quite understandable that we will naturally look for a sense of ourselves from any place that we can find it. And what better place to look than to our experiences?

> *We identify not just with our past but also with the stories that we make up about all of our life experiences including the things that we expect to happen or fear will happen to us in the future.*

The Collapse of Awareness into Identification with Our Stories, Expectations and Reactions

This phenomenon is called identification. It means getting the sense of who or what you are from anything other than what you truly are.

> *The ego is made up of a plethora of identifications. Each one of which is structured out of a story about something that has happened, something you expect to happen or something you fear or hope will happen.*

None of these things actually exist in the now. All of them are made up in our minds. This means that they are not real. They don't actually exist anywhere except in the mind.

But there's more to it than this.

Each story, memory, expectation or projection has some kind of emotional charge to it either subtle or not so subtle.

This emotional charge is a field of energy in our bodies that radiates outward from us and fills up our environment like a cloud or aura. Our awareness is collapsed inside of this field of energy, making an expectation or projection feel very real. When you are living inside the energy field of your expectations, projections and reactions it all feels like reality, even though it doesn't exist anywhere in "real life" except in your mind. We are completely unaware that we've created illusions that we live inside of because it all feels so real. It continues to feel real until we have the experience of life showing up not like our story about how it was "supposed to" show up, but simply as it actually is. When this happens it is typically upsetting because our expectation didn't get met. What's wrong with the universe? Why can't the universe get it together and show up the way that I want it too? We are disappointed, angry, frustrated, or resentful. It may help you to notice that all of these emotions are created about things that never even existed in the first place!

When we create an expectation or projection of some kind of outcome onto the future, either positive or negative, we are making up a story and then living inside of this story. What does it actually mean to be living inside of the story?

The story that we make up is a story about how we want life to happen. Because we want it to happen in a particular way we live our life expecting that it will happen this way. Even though the story is made up and isn't actually what is happening in life, because we want it to happen so badly, we begin to go about our life as if the story was actually true. So for example, if you have the idea that someone you are going to ask out on a date is going to accept your invitation you may daydream about going out with them and having a great time. You might even make reservations for two at your favorite restaurant. You might get your hair cut or buy some new clothes to wear on the date. But then the person doesn't accept your invitation because they have another commitment. The story that you made up and then lived inside of was only in your mind and not in reality. You made up a story that something would happen and you lived inside of this story as if it were going to be true but it wasn't.

When we create an expectation, the expectation is a story about what we want to have happen. Because expectations are stories made up in our mind and therefore they don't really exist anywhere except in the mind, there is an innate potential for them not to happen. It seems that there is a part of us that somehow knows this and is already prepared to have an emotional reaction to the expectation not being met. Just like when we project a possible negative outcome onto the future, we create the fear that the negative outcome will actually happen.

Emotions are fields of energy created in the body that also radiate out into the environment creating a field of energy like a cloud or aura. If you doubt that this is so, be patient and you will soon be guided through the experience of feeling the energy field of an emotion and experiencing it creating an aura of energy that radiates outside of your body.

Because the energy fields of our emotions radiate out into our environment and we experience this energy all around us, we live inside of the energy field. This makes it seem like the expectation or projection is very real, in fact, compellingly real. It is as if we are projecting a hologram out into the environment like a huge IMAX movie being shown on the screen of the environment that surrounds us. It is interesting that we even call the phenomenon of having a story about something that might happen in the future, a "projection." Most people spend their lives living in an unreal world inside the energetic movies of the stories made up in their minds and projected out into their personal environment.

The problem is that because we are identified with our projections and expectations, we are so absorbed in the illusions that we create, that this phenomenon serves as a major barrier to experiencing our essential nature, Pure Awareness. In order to experience Pure Awareness we have to be present and living in the reality of the moment, not lost to the illusions of our stories.

It is very useful to know that when our awareness is collapsed inside the identifications that make up our ego that we are living inside of energy fields that we are creating. This insight makes it possible to have new techniques for extracting our awareness from its collapse inside of the energy fields of all these identifications. The technique for escaping the illusions of identification is called the SEE Technique – Side Entrance Expansion. The SEE Technique is an experiential way of coming out of the grip of the energy field of the emotions associated with our identifications. It's actually quite easy to extract ourselves

from the false identification of who we think we are. It is just that we have never been guided in how to do it. Our parents and teachers didn't know how to do this. They were also absorbed in their own identifications, and no one ever showed them how either.

You can learn how to systematically dismantle the identifications that create your ego by learning and using the SEE Technique. Whenever you use the SEE Technique you will liberate yourself from the illusions created by the stories and learn first hand that the stories are merely expectations and projections.

The SEE Technique — Side Entrance Expansion

"After splitting up with my partner I was feeling a sense of loss and loneliness. I was stuck in a feeling of being unloved. I wanted so much to have the feeling that people loved me. When Tom guided me through the SEE Technique the energy field of the loneliness seemed like it filled up my whole universe. I had been living inside the feeling of longing for love and feeling lonely my whole life. It seemed like it was just a part of who I was."

89

"Doing the SEE Technique was utterly amazing! When I got out past the outer edge of the energy of the feeling and experienced Pure Awareness, the energy of the feeling of loneliness just faded away and was gone. I couldn't believe it. But when Tom asked me to think of the issue of needing to be loved and feeling lonely I just started to laugh. The whole thing had become ridiculous. I was so grounded in the expansive state of Pure Awareness I realized that I am LOVE. It wasn't an intellectual idea. It's a pure experience of being - of experiencing myself as universal love. I was laughing because the whole thing had become a "non-issue." You don't need to look for love outside of yourself when you have access to Pure Awareness. So now I am really free to love myself and love others without needing it. This feels so incredibly profound and liberating."

– Dezi Koster

The Energy Fields of Identifications

I'll first give you an explanation of the SEE Technique and how to do it. I will then give you a link to access audio examples on the Internet or you can practice the SEE Technique by having someone guide you through it by reading the script.

The simplest way to begin to understand the SEE Technique is to think of a situation where you expected life to happen in a certain way and it didn't. Because it didn't happen the way you wanted it to you had an emotional reaction. You reacted because your expectation didn't get met. Whatever your reaction - anger, disappointment, sadness, frustration - it is important here to notice that the emotion can be experienced as a sensation of energy in and around your body. The sensation is simple to identify because if there were not any energy to the emotion you would not be "feeling" it.

Once you can feel the emotion of your reaction allow yourself to feel where the energy of the emotion is coming from in your body. You may find it in your chest, belly or throat but it could be anywhere. You may not even be able to identify where it is coming from. That's OK too.

Notice that the emotion is a field of energy. If you allow yourself to notice the entire field of the energy of this emotional reaction you will find that it is not only located in your body but it also radiates outward into your environment surrounding your body. It probably feels like it is all around you, engulfing you like an aura or bubble.

Typically we don't allow ourselves to feel the whole energy field of our emotions. This is due to the conditioning that I described earlier as the Core Dynamic of *Resisting Feeling Things Fully*. In fact some people learn to become disassociated from the emotional energy. You may have developed a habit of going into your mind to try to figure something out like why you feel this way or how could something like this happen. However we want to distinguish our thoughts about the emotion from the sensation of the emotion in and around the body. For now, our interest is in the sensation of the emotion that is the experience of its energy field.

If you allow yourself to feel the entire field of the energy that your body is creating in its reaction to your unmet expectation, you may find that sometimes the energy field is quite large. It may extend outward from your body quite far. It may even be bigger than the room you are in; sometimes it is bigger than the entire world. When the identification has been there for a very long time and the issue is very self-defining, the energy field can sometimes seem like it is filling up your entire apparent universe.

But this energy field is occurring inside of your awareness. No matter how big the field of the energy is, it is always contained within your awareness. If the energy field really overwhelmed your entire field of consciousness you would be unconscious. But you are conscious. You are reading this book and you are aware. Even when you are experiencing the field of energy of your reaction to your unmet expectation, you are aware. And it is your awareness that is making it possible to have that experience.

So when you do the SEE Technique you allow your awareness to expand. You will remember from doing the AGAPE Technique that you could take your awareness all the way out to the outer edge of the universe. This was a great preparation for the SEE Technique. Now you are already experienced at allowing your awareness to expand outward from your body and allowing it to experience Pure Awareness filling up the entire universe.

The difference now is that you are starting from being inside of an energy field that is emanating from your body. In the SEE Technique you are simply noticing how large the energy field is by allowing your awareness to expand outward from your body, just noticing if the energy of the emotional reaction is still there.

As you allow your awareness of the energy field to continue to expand what you are looking for is the outer edge of the field of energy. When you come to the outer edge of the energy field you will be able to sense some quietness just beyond the edge. This quietness is your own awareness that is allowing you to have this experience. It is the silent background in which the energy field is occurring. It is the same silent background of Pure Awareness that you experienced during the GAP Technique.

As you allow your awareness to notice the quietness out beyond the outer edge, you will begin to get a clear distinction between the energy field of the emotion and the silent background that contains it. In the moment that this distinction becomes clear you have extracted your awareness from being collapsed inside of the energy field.

As you let your awareness notice the depth of the quietness outside the energy field of the emotion, the distinction between the energy of the emotion, and the background of silence in which the energy of the emotion is occurring, will become increasingly clear.

The SEE Technique is in fact a variation on the GAP Technique because we are looking off to the side of our experiences to sense the silence in which these experiences are happening. But when you are caught up in an emotional reaction to an unmet expectation or you are projecting a possible negative outcome onto the future, it is very difficult to find the background of silence. In fact, your awareness tends to be so absorbed in the reaction that to find the background of silence, you have to take your awareness out to the outer edge of the energy field of the reaction. Then you can access the background of silence that is the quietness that surrounds the energy field. As this is the opposite of what we are conditioned to do, which is to stay inside the energy field of our reaction, virtually no one has ever had this experience before.

It is important to make clear that you can't get there with your intellect. You can't get there by thinking about it. It is an experience not a thought. This is experiential not intellectual. When you are experientially collapsed inside the energy field of your reaction you can't get out with your intellect. The energy isn't intellectual and just understanding that you are creating the energy in response to your reaction to an unmet expectation isn't going to liberate you from the energy field.

It may be of value or interest to understand that the energy is being created due to your identification with your expectation or projection but that understanding won't bring you back to the experience of Pure Awareness. You have to allow yourself to experience the entire energy field so that you can access the quietness out beyond the edge. This then experientially extracts your awareness from being collapsed inside the energy field and also extracts you from being identified with your expectation or projection.

What happens as you allow yourself to notice the background of silence in which the energy is occurring is that you begin to notice the vastness of Pure Awareness. It has no boundaries. It is limitless. And because Pure Awareness is the essential nature of what you truly are, when you experience it, the illusory nature of the story that you created that became your expectation and reaction no longer can maintain the appearance of being real. You are no longer collapsed inside of it. Because it can no longer maintain its appearance of being real, it simply starts to shrink back into the nothingness from which you created it. It can be valuable to notice from a place of Pure Awareness that the reaction that you were inside of was a reaction to an unmet expectation. It may also be useful to notice that the story at the basis of the expectation was something that you made up in your mind. It wasn't real. It didn't actually exist anywhere other than in your mind. The energy field that you created and that you had been living inside of is what made it seem real.

It also may be valuable to simply notice that you were generating a huge field of energy in response to a story that wasn't even real. Is the creation of stories like this and the emotional reactions associated with them really something useful to you? Is there any real value or benefit to doing this? Is this the way that you want to be using your life energy? Of course not!

One kind of expectation that is worth mentioning is the expectation of a possible negative outcome. This is something that you are afraid may happen in the future. We call this projecting a possible negative outcome onto the future. This is slightly different than an unmet expectation because it hasn't happened yet. However, the fear that is being generated has the same characteristic of being an emotional energy generated out of a story about something that doesn't exist in this moment. It's another story that you are making up in your mind. So whether the emotional energy is a reaction to an unmet expectation, or it is being created as the fear of a projection of a possible negative outcome onto the future, these are both candidates for using the SEE Technique to extract yourself from being lost inside of the emotions connected to these unreal stories.

In either case, when you have expanded your awareness to notice the quietness out beyond the outer edge of the energy field of the emotional reaction the reaction will simply fade away. Recognizing that the energy is a reaction to an unreal story will help you to let go of the conditioning that created this story in the first place. You may find, as with the GAP Technique that it is initially easier to go through the SEE Technique with a guide. This section has been set up like the section on the GAP Technique so that someone can easily read the script below and guide you through using the SEE Technique. If you'd like to hear me explain the SEE Technique and guide some people through it there is an audio recording available on the **Internet at – www.thepowerofhow.com/SEE-SANYAMA-GPS.html**

How to Do the SEE Technique

The SEE Technique begins by you identifying a reaction to an unmet expectation or identifying an emotion like fear associated with a projection of some possible negative outcome onto the future. Again, it is done with the eyes closed. Once you can feel the energy of the emotion in or around your body then you allow yourself to simply notice how big the energy field of the emotion is.

Now have someone read the following script:

"Notice that the emotion that you are feeling has a field of energy to it."

Pause

"Now allow yourself to notice that the field of energy radiates out from your body creating a cloud or aura of energy all around you."

Pause

"Simply allow yourself to notice how big the energy field of the emotion is. Sometimes the field can be pretty big."

Pause

"Now, notice that the field of energy of the emotion has an outer limit. It may extend beyond your physical body, but it doesn't go on forever. There is an outer edge of the energy field that might be very well defined or kind of vague. What we are looking for is the area where the energy fades away into quietness."

Pause

"Notice where the outer edge of the energy field of the emotion is, and that there is nothing else beyond it."

Pause

Can you sense the quietness out beyond the outer edge of the energy field of the emotion?

Pause - If they can't yet sense the quietness or they have not yet noticed the outer edge of the energy field, then say

"Just keep allowing your awareness to expand more and more in order to notice the entire field of the energy until you find the outer edge and the quietness beyond it."

Pause

"Now take your awareness a little further beyond the outer edge of the emotion and notice that there is some quietness there."

Pause - Once they can sense the quietness out beyond the outer edge of the field of energy of the emotion, then say

"Now go even further from the outer edge of the emotion more deeply into the quietness that surrounds the field of its energy."

Pause

"Notice that this quietness surrounding the energy of the emotion is much bigger than the emotion itself."

Pause

"Now notice that this quietness is actually a background of silence in which the emotion is occurring."

Pause

"Notice that this background of silence doesn't have any limits. Notice how, from the perspective of the vastness of the silent background, your story, the expectation and the reaction don't seem to have as much grip on you as they did before."

Pause

"Now just allow yourself to be in the vastness of the silent background, until there is nothing left of the energy of the emotion or the expectation. It wasn't real to begin with. Enjoy the profound feeling of freedom that comes from experiencing that your expectation and reaction were just illusions."

Pause

"When the energy of the emotion is completely gone you can open your eyes."

Pause until the eyes are open and the person is back with you again.

After you have completed the SEE Technique it is good to check to see if your emotional reaction is completely resolved. You can do this by reviewing the issue that caused the initial reaction. Think about what it was and just notice if there is any emotional reaction left or not. If there is, you may need to do the SEE Technique again, going out to the outer edges and beyond the edges into the quietness of Pure Awareness. Sometimes there may be several closely related issues or expectations, each one of which has an emotional reaction to it. You can use the SEE Technique on the emotional energy field of each issue.

When you check in to see if there is any emotional reaction or projection left after the energy has faded back into nothingness, you will typically find that it is completely gone. And you have no inclination to bring it back. It is common when checking in to see if there's any reaction left that you may feel that having had the expectation in the first place was actually kind of ridiculous. The illusory nature of the story and the reaction become so obvious when looked at from the state of Pure Awareness. Many people laugh at the notion of ever again creating such a ludicrous story and reaction.

It is also good to know that sometimes there can also be one or more incomplete emotional experiences from the past that need to be resolved using the CORE Technique which you will learn a little later in the book. If this is the case, you can switch from the SEE Technique to the CORE Technique once you have learned it. This is a very potent combination. I've yet to come across an emotional energy that could not be resolved using the SEE Technique, the CORE Technique or a combination of both.

Why the SEE Technique Works So Well for Debugging Your Identifications

The reason that the SEE Technique is so effective is that in the moment that you take your awareness outside of the energy field of the emotion, you liberate your awareness from being absorbed inside the illusion created by the expectation. This is because when you bring your awareness out into the background of silence of awareness itself, you then have the direct experience of your essential nature.

Because your own awareness is what you really are, the illusion that the story that you made up in your mind is real can't maintain the appearance of being real when directly experienced side by side with the reality of your own awareness. Thus the energy of the illusion of your story and reaction simply fade away into nothing.

Using the SEE Technique to Breakthrough the Energy of Disassociation

A very useful application of the SEE Technique is to help you come out of the experience of being disassociated from your feelings. Sometimes we check out, numb out or withdraw in order to not be overwhelmed by some intense experience. This is a natural survival response and is entirely appropriate when it is needed. Going into a state of shock is an extreme example of this. It is the body's way of protecting itself.

However sometimes the disassociation can last longer than necessary and you just feel disconnected from your feelings in general. The SEE Technique can work very well with this kind of disassociation. In this case you need to allow yourself to feel the energy field of the disassociation. That might seem like a strange idea but the disassociation does have an energy field to it and actually it will be quite familiar to you if you have been experiencing disassociation. When you use the SEE Technique on the disassociation energy you may be surprised when you get to the outer edge of the energy field. I'll give you a couple of examples to make this clear.

I was teaching a seminar on the Core Dynamics and Pure Awareness Techniques in Germany in the spring of 2008. My host asked me if I would please work with a friend who was attending the seminar and use her for a demonstration in the class. He mentioned that she had

had several traumas and needed some help. Of course I was happy to do that.

As we started the session the woman explained that she had experienced three sudden traumas in a span of just a few weeks. The first was that she was in an airplane that nearly crashed but pulled up just at the last moment. She certainly thought she was going to die. The second one was her father, who she was very close to, died. The third one was that her cat that she had had for many, many years and loved dearly also died.

This woman explained that she could feel the pain of the loss of her cat and was very sad about that, but that she just couldn't feel any feelings about the near plane crash or about her father's death. She said that she knew that she must have some feelings about these events but she couldn't access them. She was disassociated from her feelings.

We first used the CORE Technique to resolve the sadness about the loss of her cat and within a few minutes the sadness was gone and she just felt her love for her cat.

Then we prepared to use the SEE Technique to resolve the energy of the disassociation. I asked her if she was prepared to feel the feelings that would be available when she let go of the disassociation. She said she was ready and willing to do that. So we started.

As soon as I asked her to go out to the outer edges of the disassociation energy field she burst into tears. She had taken her awareness out to the outer edge of the energy of the disassociation very quickly and was then able to access the pain that the disassociation had previously been masking. Now she could feel the pain of the loss of her father. She cried for a little while, and when she settled down, I had her do the CORE Technique on the energy of her the grief about her father. Again within a short time she felt much better and the sadness was gone. She did the same for the energy of the terror that she could also now access and feel about the near plane crash. Finally all of the energies of these traumas were completed and resolved. She was beaming and happy. She must have thanked me about ten times that day.

In another case, a man in Vancouver, Canada who attended a presentation I gave had been in a car accident several years before. He was the husband of one of my Master Core Dynamics Coaches and his wife asked if I could help him. He said that he felt, since the accident that he was living above and behind his body, looking down on himself. He was disassociated.

We did the SEE Technique on his energy of disassociation and as he got to the outer edge of the energy field he started laughing uncontrollably. After quite a long time of laughing he stopped but shortly after started laughing again. When he finally settled down I asked him what he was experiencing. He said that coming out of the disassociation was such a huge relief that he couldn't help but laugh and laugh. He laughed again several times over the next half hour. He said that this was extraordinary because he couldn't recall the last time he had laughed at all. His wife was thrilled and he was happy.

The main thing to be aware of when using the SEE Technique on the energy of disassociation is that when you get to the outer edge of the energy field of the disassociation there may be some surprise in store for you. Sometimes the energy of things that have been suppressed by the disassociation will burst forth because now you have access to them. Just be prepared to shift to the CORE Technique if needed. Like the woman in Germany, you may need to experience crying or some other reaction for a bit before shifting to the CORE Technique. As you will learn in the section on the CORE Technique we normally don't encourage crying but rather we guide the person to go into the center of the energy that they are experiencing. However, sometimes when coming out of disassociation and being hit in the face so to speak with the full force of the suppressed emotions there isn't any option but to allow the crying to happen. It will pass soon enough and you can then shift to the CORE or the SEE Technique as appropriate.

Remembering to Use the SEE Technique

As with all of the Pure Awareness Techniques the key is remembering to actually do the technique. One good way to learn to do the SEE Technique whenever it is needed is to work with a Certified Core Dynamics Coach. All certified Core Dynamics Coaches are highly skilled at guiding you through all eight of the Pure Awareness Techniques. After being guided through the SEE Technique several times, you will naturally develop a sense of confidence in doing it on your own. You will also start to get a feel for the kinds of situations for which it is best used and helpful.

The SEE Technique can be used to dismantle any identification. The key to success will be to be able to get in touch with the energy of each emotion associated with each particular identification. The most common kinds of identifications, and the easiest ones to find, are the emotional energy of projections of possible negative outcomes onto the future and expectations that something will happen or not happen in a particular way. When you are identified with a projection of a possible negative outcome onto the future the emotion will likely be fear. When you have an expectation, the emotion that is already present when you create the expectation, will typically be disappointment, anger, frustration, sadness, etc. Whatever the emotion, typically all you have to do to get in touch with it is to imagine the expectation not being met and you will be able to feel your potential reaction. If it is a projection of a possible negative outcome onto the future all you need to do is think about the possibility of that negative outcome actually happening and you will very likely get in touch with the fear. Once you can feel the field of energy of the emotion, then do the SEE Technique to extract your awareness from its collapse inside the illusion that is creating this emotional energy. The emotional energy will fade away into nothing. Once it has faded away it usually doesn't come back because you become so completely clear that it was just a story that you made up. It doesn't actually exist. The apparent reality of it will not seem real any more and you'll be free of being stuck inside of this particular illusion. Use the SEE Technique any time you feel caught in the grip of an emotion. If it doesn't seem to work use the CORE Technique. With these two tools you can liberate yourself from the grip of any emotion.

How Using the SEE Technique Impacts Your Life

The SEE Technique has an enormous potential to impact your life in ways that you may not have even been able to imagine. Each time you do the SEE Technique you are dismantling a piece of your illusory, false sense of self that is called your ego. As you continue to use it, more and more you will find yourself recognizing when you are about to create an expectation or when you are starting to create a story of projecting a possible negative outcome onto the future. You'll simply stop doing these things. The uselessness of expectations and projections and their associated emotional reactions will become increasingly obvious to you to the point where you will simply stop creating these illusory stories. This will increasingly free you to be fully present in the moment rather than caught up in the illusions created by the stories.

> *When you are present you are in Pure Awareness. In Pure Awareness there is no ego, there is only the totality of your own awareness ready to respond to the needs of each moment with the fullness of your Being. This is a life worth living.*

It is living in the zone. You've probably had glimpses of this state of being when you are doing something that just flows effortlessly and it almost seems like you aren't even doing it. It happens in sports. It happens during creative projects. It can happen anytime. But what is truly wonderful is when it is the way that you experience life every moment of every day. It may sound unreal or fantastic to think that this could be a living reality but this is only because you've been mainly living life with only rare experiences of being in the zone. Now, by using the SEE Technique at every opportunity you can rapidly dismantle your identifications, expectation, and projections so that you live life in the zone more and more until it becomes your constant reality.

The WONDER Technique —Wait On Neutral During Emotional Reactions

"It took me a little while to understand the WONDER Technique. I got the idea of unplugging the power cord or shifting to neutral. That made sense to me. But remembering to do it was the challenge for me. What made the difference for me was when I was able to get some help from a Core Dynamics Coach who

guided me through the SEE Technique for my habit of criticizing myself. Before, I would just be really down on myself for not living up to my own expectations. After doing the SEE Technique it was just like Tom said. I was now much more aware of my tendency to be down on myself. Then when I would feel the old tendency to have those kinds of thoughts it was really easy to unplug from them. Now they just don't come up anymore. I feel great about me pretty much all the time."

– Michael Harlow

[Although Michael passed away in 2008 he told me sometime before his death that his life had been deeply enriched by learning and practicing the Pure Awareness Techniques. I include his comments here as a memorial to a great guy who was also a great Core Dynamics Coach.]

The WONDER Technique is for helping you stop doing things that are driven by conditioned responses. When you are caught up in most conditioned behaviors you tend to not be living in Pure Awareness. The WONDER Technique is also to help you break habits that you no longer want to have. It involves noticing the old behavior when it is about to happen and then instead of allowing it to happen, simply stop giving energy to that particular thought or action. However, in order to do this, you have to have enough awareness that you can notice that you are about to think or do the conditioned behavior. The key is to first have enough awareness to notice that the old behavior is about to happen, and then to choose to stop giving that behavior any energy. The result is that nothing happens and instead of becoming absorbed in a conditioned response you can simply settle back into Pure Awareness. If the direct experience of Pure Awareness has been lost you can use one of the other Pure Awareness Techniques to bring your awareness back to it. The WONDER Technique is a Pure Awareness Technique because it quickly brings you back to the experience of Pure Awareness on the fly, in the moment. Doing the WONDER Technique is like taking a very quick plunge into the GAP.

The WONDER Technique is also known as "unplugging the power cord" or "shifting to neutral." These analogies capture the essence of this technique. Imagine you are driving a car on a level road and you shift it into neutral. What happens? You coast to a stop.

If you are using a vacuum cleaner and unplug the power cord while it's running, what happens? You hear the motor wind down and stop. In both of these analogies the principle concept is that you stop feeding energy into the system. When there's no energy nothing happens.

If cultivating a state in which you live from Pure Awareness all the time is starting to sound appealing to you, then learning and practicing the WONDER Technique is going to be another great tool to help you to do just that. Remember that the two primary barriers to enjoying the presence of Pure Awareness in our lives all of the time are our identifications many of which include habitual conditioned responses (our habits) and our incomplete emotional experiences from the past that we hold in our bodies. You'll be learning the CORE Technique and the GPS Technique a bit later. These are the tools for completing the incomplete experiences from the past.

The WONDER Technique is another wonder-ful tool for eliminating unwanted habitual conditioned responses. We could also consider WONDER to be the starting point of most of the other Pure Awareness Techniques because you have to be aware enough of the old way of being (conditioning) so that you can unplug from it and do whichever of the Pure Awareness Techniques that best dismantles the conditioned response. One of the reasons that we use the word WONDER for the acronym for this technique is that when we wonder about something, it means that we are being aware of it and curious about it at the same time. We bring our awareness to the present moment. Being aware is the key. Being aware of something is much different than simply reacting automatically from conditioning which is more of an unconscious, unaware process.

The WONDER Technique is the process of disallowing energy to be fed into thoughts and actions that would normally occur by default, by habit, as learned conditioned responses. For example, when someone cuts you off on the freeway, a common conditioned response is to swear at the other driver or have some other related reaction of upset. Or, any time that you are impulsive, like purchasing something that you really don't need or want but you are doing it under some kind of pressure like a sale or some urgency created by a salesman you are reacting with a conditioned response.

It is also important to know that the more you do the SEE and CORE Techniques the more you will have enough awareness to be able to unplug or shift to neutral from all sorts of things. The Wonder Technique is very useful for situations where all that is needed is to "unplug," to return to neutral, to Pure Awareness.

How to do the WONDER Technique

The words for each letter of our acronym WONDER - Wait On Neutral During Emotional Reactions describes what you actually do to use the WONDER Technique. Think of it like this. When you are about to do something that is an expression of a habit that you want to eliminate it begins with the inception of a thought. Nothing can happen without having a thought to do it. So the mechanism of any habit is always Thought – Action. But with habits, the awareness of the first step, having the thought, has typically become unconscious.

In the case of conditioned responses and habitual thoughts and actions, you have become so skilled at doing that particular action that you have become unconsciously competent at doing it. You've become so good at it that you aren't even aware of the thought part of the formula any more.

There are four stages to the learning process, whether it is learning to ride a bike, tie our shoes or play the piano. Before we learn to do something, like tying our shoes, we don't know how to do it and someone has to do it for us. We don't even know that we can't do it. It's not even an option for us. This stage of the learning process is called unconscious incompetence.

At the point at which we begin to try to tie our shoes it takes a lot of concentration and effort. We may not even get it right for a while. This is the stage of learning called conscious incompetence. We know that we can't do it but we are practicing and working towards the next stage.

When we are successful at tying our shoes we have reached the stage called conscious competence. Now we know how to do it but it still takes thought and paying attention in order to do it properly.

The fourth stage of the learning process is when tying our shoes becomes so familiar and we have done it so many times that we no longer have to think about it. It has become automatic. It's as if our shoes just get tied. It's almost like they tie themselves now. It's effortless and we don't even think about it. We have now reached the stage of learning called unconscious competence.

So habitual behaviors are the ones at which we have become unconsciously competent. Feeding energy into the habitual behavior is so deeply conditioned in us that we don't even realize any more that we are the ones who are feeding the thoughts and actions of the habit with energy. If the habit no longer serves us as in our habits based on the Core Dynamics of Human Conditioning then we have become the victims of our own unconscious competence at doing that habit.

One of the ways you can use the WONDER Technique is to target each individual unwanted habit that you have become unconsciously competent at. You can start by making a list of all of the habits that you want to dismantle. It's unlikely that you will remember to do the WONDER Technique for all of them at once. I suggest that when you make your list you can then prioritize the list and take the highest priority habit or type of conditioned or impulsive behavior and adopt one or more of the strategies described below. These strategies will help you be aware that you are about to engage in that kind of thought or behavior and then ou cam unplug from it.

In order to be aware enough of the habit so that you can change it, you have to interrupt the thought-action mechanism to give you time to make the decision to NOT feed the old thoughts and actions with energy anymore. After all, if you don't give them energy they simply don't happen anymore. The trick is to get good at noticing the inception of the thought that is about to rear its ugly head out of nothingness and sweep you away into automatic pilot habit land.

By practicing the other Pure Awareness Techniques regularly and often you deepen your experience of Pure Awareness so that you are more and more aware all the time. When you increase your natural capacity of being aware, you can unplug from any habitual or impulsive type of thought or action easily.

You can also think of the WONDER Technique as a clean up method once you have done the SEE Technique or the CORE Technique for a given emotional reaction or incompletion. If there is any residual reactivity left or if there is even just a tendency to do something that you used to do by default that you no longer want to do, you will have enough awareness of the issue after doing the SEE or CORE Technique that you will be able to successfully notice it coming and unplug from it.

Creating a Gap between Stimulus and Response (Habit Interrupter)

I remember once in the early 90's when I was waiting between flights in the Chicago O'Hare airport. I decided to browse through a bookstore while I was waiting. As I did one book almost literally jumped off of the shelf into my hands. It was Stephen Covey's now famous The Seven Habits of Highly Effective People. Well of course I bought it and took it with me to read on the plane. As I devoured this classic work I was intrigued with many of the concepts. One point that I have thought about over the years in particular that relates to our current topic was the idea that in the gap between stimulus and response we have freedom of choice. Since first reading this idea I have given it quite a lot of thought. What I have noticed is that so much of the time our actions are so quick and reactive that there isn't enough of a gap to be able to have the option of a choice. Having a gap would mean that there is an awareness, a kind of observing of what is about to happen.

The question then becomes, how can we create a big enough gap, or how can we expand and enhance our awareness of the gap between stimulus and response. We need enough awareness of the gap between stimulus and response that we actually do have the freedom to chose whether or not to allow energy to flow into a thought and turn into an action. This is very important because without enough awareness of a gap between stimulus and response there is no freedom of choice. You are just being the product of your learned behaviors, your conditioned responses.

So often the reaction is so automatic that we don't recognize that we are reacting habitually until we are already into the reaction or even after the fact. Often our conditioned responses are so fast that there's just not much of a gap between stimulus and response at all. When this is the case we find ourselves doing the habit without realizing it in time to unplug. So the real issue always boils down to awareness. We have to have enough awareness of the gap between stimulus and response to be at choice. In fact the gap between stimulus and response IS awareness itself.

This means that in order to notice the gap between stimulus and response we need to increase awareness. This is precisely what practicing the Pure Awareness Techniques does. So the ability to be able to notice the gap between stimulus and response can greatly increase by practicing these techniques. All of this means that freedom of choice is something that can be systematically improved. Just understanding the concept of the gap between stimulus and response is an important distinction. But now the Pure Awareness Techniques allow this distinction to become a practical reality.

Once awareness has been developed enough that you do become

aware of the gap between stimulus and response, the Pure Awareness Technique to use is WONDER. You simply notice the old response about to rear its head out of nothingness and disallow energy to be fed into it.

So far I have discovered three ways to develop increased awareness. I refer to these as habit interrupters. The first two are cognitive interrupters and the third, which is by far the most amazing and effective one, is an energetic interrupter. Here are the traditional cognitive ones that are very good:

1. Making a list. Here's the sequence of what you do:

- Make a list of the habits that you want
  to dismantle.

- Prioritize them and start with the one that you feel is your
  top priority.

- Consciously unplug from engaging in that habit every time it
  comes up.

- Carry a small notepad with you during the day and write
  down every time the habit comes up and what you did
  about it.

- Put your attention on noticing just this one habit and decide
  that you are going to begin to catch it earlier and earlier
  in the process of noticing when the thought that turns
  into the action of this habit is about to manifest out of the
  nothingness of your awareness.

- In making the list, choose the highest priority habit to change and make the decision to start noticing the process of how this habit manifests from nothingness, to thought, to action, and make a note of what happens each time the old habit comes up. This can help to begin to create enough awareness specific to this particular habit that you can unplug the power cord and stop feeding energy into it.

2. Use pictures or written reminders to interrupt the habit. You very likely already know about this one as it's commonly recommended by lots of personal development experts:

- You put post-it notes on your mirror to remind you to notice and not do the habit. You put a note in your wallet. You put a post-it note on the side of your computer screen. You put a reminder to notice the habit you are changing (encoded in some way to save your privacy about it if need be) as a message on the screen saver of your computer.

- You can use a picture of what you will be like (such as a picture of someone who is slender if your habit is over eating) and put it on the screensaver or on the door of your refrigerator as a habit interrupter.

- Get creative and design or find physical reminders that will help you to notice and be more aware that you are about to engage in the old habit before you just find yourself doing it again.

You get the idea. These are good standard methods of habit interrupters.

The last one to mention is new and was developed as a part of the emerging field of Human Software Engineering. It functions as an interrupter of conditioned responses at the deeper level of energy and information that tends to hold these habits in place.

3. Use a Human Software Engineering™ device such as the WaveMaker™ or WaveMaker Pro™ to debug your inner human software and cancel out the pattern of energy that holds the habit in place.

- The WaveMaker and the WaveMaker Pro are new technologies of the emerging field of Human Software Engineering (HSE). They are designed to pick up the ultra-fine electromagnetic field patterns of energy and information from the body, electronically invert them and send them back to the body via cables and "connectors" (our Human Software Engineering term for electrodes).

- These HSE Technologies use a sophisticated application of the principle of wave interference from physics. They work in a similar but greatly expanded way to noise canceling headsets. Like a noise canceling headset, these HSE devices cancel out the wave patterns of energy but instead of canceling out the energy patterns of the noise from the environment they cancel out the energy of the "noise" of our conditioning held in our bodies.

- The WaveMaker and the WaveMaker Pro represent major breakthroughs in the application of the principle of wave theory from physics to the fields of personal development, coaching, spiritual development and human potential. They also have applications in health care, addiction recovery and other fields. For more information about these extraordinary new technologies see the appendix for links to the Internet.

- I have found that when the underlying basis of people's habits gets debugged using wave interference, often the habit just disappears. Other times the debugging opens up a much bigger gap of awareness between you and the old default habitual reaction. This means that it now becomes much, much easier to notice that the habit is about to express itself automatically and to unplug instead, shift to neutral and not allow energy to be fed into the habit. Without energy it doesn't manifest and all that is left is Pure Awareness.

Eliminating Conditioned Responses

What we are after is to eliminate our conditioned responses so that we can enjoy living in Pure Awareness without the periods of being lost to our conditioning. To facilitate this the penetrating insights of the 12 Core Dynamics of Human Conditioning can be very useful. When you learn the nature of the conditioning at the basis of each of the Core Dynamics, you gain a new kind of awareness of the real basis of your behaviors. You really start to understand the nature of your conditioning. You'll begin to see in great detail how your preverbal conditioning caused you to make "feeling level decisions" about yourself, your relationships to people and to your experiences and interactions with the world around you.

Once you understand the Core Dynamics model and become aware of specific expressions of a particular core dynamic that is causing habitual conditioned "reactive" responses you can decide to become a master of the following steps:

- First practice becoming aware of every conditioned response as it begins to arise in you.

- Unplug the power or shift to neutral.

- Notice when you are beginning to react with a conditioned response as opposed to a conscious choice. You can disallow the thought to continue to receive any energy/power if you are aware of it before it launches into speech or action. The reactive conditioned thoughts are contrary to what you really want in your life.

- You must make the conscious choice to become aware of them. You are so use to these old habits being a part of your life that you won't tend to notice them unless you have made a decision to become aware of them.

- In order to catch yourself, you have to pay attention. This is where there can be a value to using the first two cognitive interrupters that are listed above. You can also arrange to get with a WaveMaker Coach and debug the energy of the unconscious competence of the habit to open up more awareness of the gap between stimulus and response.

Becoming aware of the Core Dynamic operating at the basis of your issue will help you recognize the type of conditioned responses that habitually come up in your mind. Becoming aware of this is just like unplugging the power on a CD player or an old phonograph. It just stops or winds down.

Recognize that you are the only person who is in control of which thoughts you allow to continue to receive energy. You control which emerging thoughts are allowed to actually formulate into a fully formed thought and then turn into actions, and which ones you let sink back into the nothingness from which they came. This can be very powerful and liberating.

You do not have to continue to be the victim of your own thoughts. Who gives them energy anyway? It's not someone else. Thinking that you don't have control over which thoughts you allow your awareness to energize and entertain is also a part of your conditioning. It is characteristic of the high level of unconscious competence that you have developed through a lifetime of energizing the habitual thoughts.

You don't have to be a victim of your own thoughts. You may not even know that you are. It's even more likely that you haven't known how to stop being a victim of your thoughts even if you did know that you were.

It is far more effective to shift to neutral/unplug the power than to:

- Negate the thought.

- Attempt to replace the thought with another thought.

- Dwell on the thought.

- Deride yourself for having started to think it.

As you become good at unplugging you will become increasingly aware of conditioned responses that you have been doing in the past without realizing that this was happening. As I have mentioned several times, most people live their lives as the product of their conditioning and yet don't know that this is so. This is precisely because of the lack of awareness. So mastering the ability to eliminate conditioned responses is a direct consequence of cultivating increased awareness.

In order to gain true mastery of the ability to eliminate your conditioning and live in the freedom of Pure Awareness there is another very specific approach you can take. If you make a list of the ways of being that you know that you don't like about yourself, the list of habits that you would like to break, you will find that there is some kind of identification associated with each habit. You have become a person who does that particular behavior. This means that you get part of the sense of who you are from being that way. Conditioning is closely related to identification.

This next part is a bit subtle but it can be very powerful. Here's what you can do -

Any habit is going to have an element of identification associated with it. What is needed is to find the way in which the habit is "self-defining." If you can get a sense of yourself as being a person who does this habit you may be able to get in touch with an emotion associated with the habit. An even more likely way to get in touch with the emotion associated with the habit, will be to imagine yourself being someone who doesn't do this habit, and see how that feels. You may have two feelings, one of relief or enjoyment of no longer having the habit but there will also likely be a sense that you have lost something familiar. That feeling of loss will have a sense about it - that there will be a part of you (the habit) that will be missing. It will probably be a fear that you won't know who you really are any more, if that habit were truly gone.

This fear is a candidate for the SEE Technique. You use the SEE Technique to bring your awareness to the outer edge of the energy of the fear of losing part of the sense of who you are. This allows you to come out of that fear into the reality of your own Pure Awareness. This is the very awareness needed to create the gap between stimulus and response that will give you freedom of choice. It will give you enough awareness that you can then do the WONDER Technique and unplug from your old habitual response. With practice you can master this ability to eliminate conditioned responses by first disconnecting from your identification with them by using the SEE Technique. Then shift to neutral or unplug from the habit if it ever comes up again.

One of my mentors once said, "Neutrality is the most powerful dismantler of negativity." You will be mastering the skill of eliminating conditioned responses when you have the clear awareness that every action you take is coming from Pure Awareness.

Habits—Shift to Neutral Rather than Replace Them

One commonly proposed idea in personal development books and seminars is to change a habit by replacing one habit with a different and hopefully better one. This concept is in part based on the observation that human beings are creatures of habit. There is an assumption that because we seem to be creatures of habit, that this strategy is our only real option. However, with the development of the Pure Awareness Techniques there is an upgrade to this concept.

Instead of being a creature of habit—which means being the product of your conditioning—what if you developed a state of being in which you could respond spontaneously to the needs of each moment with the fullness of your Being? What if it were possible to make decisions that were not based on past conditioning but were coming directly from Pure Awareness? What if your decisions were based on a fully present, fully conscious, perfectly appropriate response to the unique needs of each moment?

Instead of being a creature of habit how about being a creature of spontaneous right action? How about becoming a person whose decisions and actions come directly from the infinite wisdom of the field of pure intelligence, pure knowing, the field of Pure Awareness? Now that would be a major upgrade to your inner human software operating system!

Shifting from the Terror of Uncertainty to the WONDER and Delight of Uncertainty

One of the things about shifting to neutral is that in neutrality there is no external reference. When there is no reference other than Pure Awareness, which is not a "thing," you can be left feeling uncertain. We are in the habit of liking to feel certain about things. Certainty gives us a feeling of safety and security. Most people are afraid of the unknown and when you are in neutrality you are in a state of uncertainty, the land of the unknown.

It is an amazing experience to shift from being terrified of uncertainty to being totally fine with uncertainty. It's very common to be afraid of the unknown. In fact, it's so common that the very word "uncertainty" is, for most people, strongly associated with fear. This is of course due to the Core Dynamic of *Resisting Feeling Things Fully* as we are afraid that something might happen that we won't be able to handle. To make this shift in your way of being requires that you be willing to face and handle whatever shows up. And you can't just decide to do that by choosing to. You have to first resolve the fear of the unknown. This is done using the CORE or the SEE Technique or both.

What you want to achieve is a shift in your state of being from living in the terror of uncertainty to living in its WONDER and delight. In the WONDER of uncertainty anything is possible. When you live in the "terror" of uncertainty by fearing what might happen if you don't have everything figured out, you will naturally want to have some predetermined, preconditioned way of responding to give you some semblance of certainty. This is of course a false sense of security. And besides, who's to say that the predetermined way of responding is going to be optimal or even adequate for any given situation? An upgrade to this way of functioning is to be able to respond to the unique needs of each situation in life with the fullness of your being, with whatever is the most appropriate response in each moment.

In order to live in the WONDER of uncertainty so that you can respond to the needs of each moment with the fullness of your being, you will want to use the SEE and CORE Techniques frequently enough to achieve emotional mastery and confidence. It becomes important to learn to be in a state of being in which you feel completely comfortable in handling anything that may come up. That's the only way you can feel OK with uncertainty and in fact even enjoy it. This will take some practice. It requires a shift in your state of being and is a natural state when you have Pure Awareness awakened within you and present all the time. You can then enjoy the wonderful surprises that life presents to you when you can be fully present to uncertainty, and are not afraid of being overwhelmed.

When to use the WONDER Technique

- When you feel the onset of an emotional reaction.

- When you notice that you are about to energize an unwanted habit.

- When you feel impulsive.

- When you start the WAIT Technique prior to an emotional reaction. You unplug and WAIT for clarity.

- When you start the CORE or SEE Technique by unplugging from your old reactions to the emotional energy of avoidance or absorption. You have to unplug from the old way before starting the CORE or SEE Technique.

- Make the decision to stop reacting impulsively and to master the WONDER Technique.

Remembering to Use the WONDER Technique

If you follow the guidelines in the previous sections for creating more of a gap of awareness between stimulus and response, you will begin to remember to use the WONDER Technique. Understand that remembering to use the WONDER Technique is by its nature a challenge, because habits are unconsciously competent behaviors. The only way to be truly successful is to have a realistic plan for dismantling the unconscious part of it. You will have to decide to use some combination of the habit interrupters to create the gap of awareness. Only then are the WONDER Techniques of unplugging the power cord or shifting to neutral even possible.

Making the decision to adopt a plan to do this is important not only for being able to change habits that you want to change, but more importantly, this will free you to live from Pure Awareness so that all of your actions can be the expression of who and what you really are. This is so much better than a life of being the victim of your habits. It is worth the attention that it takes to do this.

How Using the WONDER Technique Impacts Your Life

It's hard to imagine a life without all of the habits and conditioned responses that you have been inadvertently perpetuating all of your life. So, like anything else, without experiencing it, you really can't know what a life like that is like. Is it worth the "work" to dismantle the old habits? Yes! Especially, if they are keeping you stuck in reactivity, struggle and suffering.

What you will notice as you begin to dismantle the habits that you want to change is that there may be a period of adjustment to being non-reactive, and simply not doing the things you have done in the past. You may find yourself feeling a sense of – I should be doing something! - but you don't have to. If there's no clear inner directive then all that is needed in the moment is to unplug, shift to neutral, and be in the WONDER of uncertainty.

You see, the WONDER Technique is also the front end of the WAIT Technique. And while you're doing the WAIT Technique you can then do the CORE, GPS, GAP, AGAPE and/or SANYAMA as you wait for clarity. They all work together to help you re-establish your direct experience of Pure Awareness and cultivate living from Pure Awareness until one day you are so grounded in it that you will never lose it again. It's a very special kind of awakening to fully know and experience that the ultimate reality of who you really are is Pure Awareness itself.

Happy unplugging!

Section 3 – How to Know that You Know

The vast majority of people live primarily from their conditioning. Personal decisions and actions are based on what they "think" they should do or on emotional reactions or moods. When you live from your conditioning it appears that you have choice and are being consciously true to yourself, but you are not. You are actually living from a false sense of yourself. However, you are unable to see that you are living from your conditioning or a false sense of self. This is because you have become so identified with your conditioning that it feels like it is a part of who you are. The problem is that living this way results in struggle and suffering. But there is another way. Rather than making decisions from your conditioning, you can make decisions from a deeper knowing, from a place of congruence and authenticity from deep within you.

Have you ever had the experience of having a desire and then forgetting about it, only to have it manifest almost like magic without you doing anything to bring it about? Pretty much everyone I've asked this question of has said yes. Isn't it great when that happens? How would you like your whole life to have this kind of effortless "in-the-zone" quality to it? Well, it's possible through learning and practicing the SANYAMA and the WAIT Techniques. Before teaching you how to use these Pure Awareness techniques I'd like to give you a context for understanding how and why they work so well.

You will recall that I mentioned earlier that the universe operates on the law of least effort. Sometimes you may appear to have a role in making something happen or it may seem like it happens without you doing anything to bring it about. But whether your body, mind and personality seem to be involved or not, these two **Pure Awareness techniques give you the tools you need to align yourself with the law of least effort.**

Many people have also had the effortless experience in their lives when they just "know" something, or they are certain about something without the benefit or logic or reason. This kind of knowing or certainty comes from deep within. For most people this kind of experience doesn't happen very often. If it does happen you may not be able to distinguish between this kind of inner knowing and your thinking mind that has been conditioned to doubt such experiences.

Due to the Core Dynamic of *Resisting Feeling Things Fully* we develop the habit of using our intellect to attempt to understand the experience with our mind. Most of us become so habituated to relying on our intellect, that when we get an experiential "knowing" from deep within we may not recognize it as our "knowing." We will likely over-ride it with thoughts or doubts about it. This causes us to not be able to make a clear distinction between thinking and knowing.

Knowing comes from having a direct experience of something, not from thinking about it or figuring it out. You may have had a kind of inner knowing about what kind of career you would have, and later in your life it turns out pretty much the way you knew it would. Or perhaps you meet someone and your sense is that you will have some kind of relationship with them, and you do. This is sometimes referred to as having an intuition or a premonition. If you've had this kind of experience you know what I am talking about. It is as if you are seeing into the future. Perhaps this is precisely what is happening.

How to Remember the Future

Quantum Physicists tell us that the mathematics of the past and the future are the same. This prompts them to ask the question - Why do we only remember the past? Actually we remember the future all the time but we are heavily conditioned to negate this kind of perception. Every time we have an intuition about something, or a desire or a feeling that something is going to happen, we are remembering the future. It's happening all the time.

How many people consistently trust and act on this kind of remembering? Not many! That's because of the Core Dynamic of Ignoring Your Intuition. When this dynamic is in play we have an experience of intuitive knowing (we remember the future) which is then immediately followed by a conditioned response of fear. Our fear is that if we trust or take action based on this "knowing" there will be some kind of negative consequence that we really don't want to face. The result is that we don't trust or act on our inner knowing, and we further ingrain the habit of not being able to make the distinction between our conditioned thinking and our inner knowing.

Because so many people can't tell the difference between an intuitive knowing kind of thought and an emotionally reactive conditioned response kind of thought, we assume that we don't remember the future and only remember the past.

Intention

Another phenomenon related to remembering the future has to do with intention. Intention is something often talked about as something that we create or do. We have an intention. We set an intention. We intend our life into reality. This is the commonly held kind of thinking that leads to the notion that I create my reality!

I propose that intentions are something we perceive. They are possible future realities that we can step into. In order to look at intention in this way we have to examine how intention comes to us.

As I mentioned earlier, knowing is based on direct experience. You can't "know" the taste of a strawberry without taking a bite of one. Therefore we use our senses to know or experience something that is as yet distant from us in time and space but already exists. We experience intentions through our senses. The formulating of the intention into words is done by our intellect, yet the words are only the representation of that which we are experiencing, not the experience itself. The formulating of an intention into words is what gives it the similarity to our other thoughts that are also structured in words. Even though both intention thoughts and conditioned response thoughts are formulated in words, the origins of these two kinds of thoughts are completely different. To understand this, we have to look more closely at our five senses and how we "sense" our intentions.

I assume that you are reading this book silently. Are you hearing the words that you are reading now with your ears? No, you are hearing them in your awareness. Imagine for a moment some place that you love to go on vacation (assuming you are not there at the moment). Imagine what it looks like to be there. Can you see it? Are you seeing these images with your eyes? No, you are seeing them in your awareness. What makes this possible? When you have a thought or see an image in your "mind's eye" you are using an aspect of your ability to hear and see with something independent of the physical sensing mechanisms of your ears and eyes. Perhaps the capacity to sense is an innate characteristic of Awareness itself and that our physical senses are perhaps only the outer and grosser expression of that capacity. This means there is an important distinction between our physical senses and our "subtle senses". Our innate ability to see, hear, taste, touch and smell is a natural characteristic of Awareness itself. Just the fact that we hear thoughts and see mental images in our mind makes it clear that the "subtle senses" are a natural part of human experience. Everyone can hear thoughts in their mind. We do it all the time.

You may have been taught to think that the body and our ability to think are the result of the chemistry that makes up the body, or that certain chemical interactions in the brain produce our thoughts. Therefore, the idea that awareness is primary, and that thoughts are not produced as a by-product of having the physical body may seem backwards to you. However, matter is made of energy, not the other way around. And I am proposing that energy is actually just the expression of awareness, not the other way around. It is not important whether you believe these ideas or not, as they are just one explanation for how it could be possible to remember the future. Fortunately the Pure Awareness Techniques will work independent of belief or even intellectual understanding of how or why they work.

Our physical senses are limited to sensing in our immediate environment. We can only see so far and hear things from a certain distance. Certainly with taste, smell and touch it is similar. The food has to touch our taste buds to register the taste, but we can also "imagine" the taste of a hot fudge sundae in our awareness (if we've tasted one in the past). Though we may not be aware of this, all five senses have subtle counterparts such as imagining a taste. I would assert that our subtle senses are innate capabilities inherent in awareness itself. The subtle senses are not limited to sensing things in our immediate environment or even in our current place in time and space. Consider that when you "see" that favorite vacation spot in your mind's eye you may not be recalling a memory stored in the brain but actually "seeing" the place with your subtle senses. In Lynn McTaggert's book, The Field,[1] she reports on recent research that strongly suggests that memory isn't actually images and sounds stored on some sort of "hard drive" in your brain. Instead the research suggests that the brain acts more like a high speed, wireless Internet connection, a technology for accessing information from "The Field." The field then includes the past and the future and all time and space. Consistent with this idea is the concept that intentions are a product of the subtle senses tuning into and experiencing a specific place in time and space, a place that we can step into as a possible future reality. We are perceiving a future reality that already exists, but we just aren't proximate to it yet in time and space so we are not yet experiencing it with our physical senses.

An analogy may help to clarify how intentions move from sensing to manifestation. Let's say that you are visiting Paris for the first time. You arrive and go to your hotel. You booked a hotel with a view of the Eiffel tower from your hotel window. But you are quite a ways across the city so although you can see the Eiffel tower, it is just a general outline of it. You know it's the tower because you have seen it in pictures, protruding up above the city as it does.

So you decide to take a nice long walk through Paris and get up close to the Eiffel tower so that you can experience it first hand. You go down to the front desk, get a map and directions of how to walk

---

1   The Field: The Quest for the Secret Force of the Universe by Lynne McTaggert, 2002, HarperCollins.

through the streets of Paris to the tower and off you go.

From down at the street level you can't see the tower any more as the view is blocked by near by buildings. As you walk in the direction of the tower you occasionally come to a place where the streets are open in just the right way so you get glimpses of the tower as you get closer to it. Each time you see it successively closer you can make out more and more of the detail. Now you can see the many crossing strips of metal, the elevators, the landings and even some little figures of people standing up on the tower.

As you get even closer, the details of the tower come into sharper and clearer view until you are right next to it and you can reach out and touch the actual metal structure with your hands. Now you are having the direct experience of the Eiffel tower up close and personal using your physical senses.

This story is analogous to what happens when we have an intention. Having the intention is a perception of something that is remote in time and space. It is something that already exists and it is a possible reality that we may step into given the right circumstances. Therefore, we are remembering the future or having a perception of a future reality. This is your awareness having a direct experience of something in the future with the subtle senses. As we know from quantum physics, time is an illusion and everything exists in the present moment. We are just moving through life inside the illusions of time and space. So any future possible reality that you might step into already exists.

If you are used to thinking of your reality as being only that which you can see, touch and perceive with your physical senses, then this idea is going to seem quite foreign and strange to you. But whether you believe it or not you are using your subtle senses all the time. Every time you have a thought, everything you remember, such as where to turn on the way to the grocery store, you are using your subtle senses to navigate through life.

Because the subtle senses are not limited by time and space, when you remember the past and the future you are using your subtle senses. This is not an ability relegated only to psychics we're talking about here. This is a natural ability that every human has. Just the fact that we hear thoughts in our mind and not in our ears makes it clear that we all have subtle senses.

The problem is that most of us are so conditioned to "think" that we have not developed the skill of being able to clearly distinguish our "made up" thoughts from our subtle sensory perceptions of the future. Perhaps those we call psychics are simply people who have developed the skill of clearly making this distinction.

Intention vs. Expectation

Remembering the Future Doesn't Necessarily Come with a Calendar

What makes it difficult to distinguish between the thoughts we make up in our mind and those subtle sensory perceptions of the future?

To understand what happens we need to look at the difference between intention and expectation. If intention is a perception or a remembering of the future, this is quite distinct from expectation. An expectation is a story that we make up in our mind and we become attached to it happening in a certain way. For most people it seems to work in the following way. We have a remembering of the future (intention) and then the mind jumps in and attempts to control when and how our intention will manifest. When we remember the future, it usually doesn't come with a calendar or a date when the intention will become reality. Sometimes it does, but for most people there isn't real clarity about when the intention that we perceive with the subtle senses, will happen or if it will actually happen at all. Like our story about taking a walk to the Eifel tower, just because we might happen to notice the Louvre on the way there doesn't necessarily mean that we will take a side trip to visit it. For that matter, just because we decide to go see the tower doesn't mean that we will arrive at a particular moment in time.

Our mind has become conditioned to jump in and set a date when we want something to happen. We may also start to attempt to dictate how it will come about. When we do this our intention converts into an expectation. And in that moment it changes from a perception of a possible future reality that we might step into, to something that only exists as a story made up in our mind. When we create an expectation we disconnect from our natural experience of perceiving what is coming and we start to live inside of a story of how we think it will be.

Intentions and expectations are uniquely different. Intentions are fluid. They evolve as we get closer to them in time and space. Just like the Eiffel tower becoming clearer as we get closer to it in our walk across Paris, our intention becomes clearer as we get closer to the time and place that we are perceiving with our subtle senses. We may find as we get closer to the experience of our intention that we might have to take a different route than we originally thought in order to get there. Similar to our walk towards the Eiffel tower, if a street that we were going to take is closed for repairs we may have to adjust our course and go around the closed street. Similarly as we approach the time and place where we will step into the physical reality of our intention we may find obstacles along the way that we couldn't see when we first had the perception of the intention, and we may have to adjust. So intentions evolve as we get closer to that possible reality that we may step into. We might even decide on the way to the Eiffel tower to take a side excursion and go to the Louvre for the day, and see the Eiffel tower on another day. If someone accompanying us had the expectation to go to the Eiffel tower they may get upset if they are attached to their expectation and it doesn't get met.

Expectations are more rigid and fixed than intentions. This is because we become attached to "our way", the way that we think things should happen. When we turn an intention into an expectation we set ourselves up for disappointment because the story that we are making up about how or when it should happen, doesn't exist anywhere other than in our mind. So it can't happen the way we expect it too because in creating the expectation we have disconnected from simply perceiving reality as it is coming to us. We are now living in a story about it rather than the increasingly clear perception of what's coming.

The other thing about expectations is that they tend to lead to emotional reactions when the expectation doesn't happen the way we want it to. The emotional reaction is embedded into the expectation at its inception. I suspect this happens because there must be some part of us that already knows that it can't happen the way we are making it up in our mind, and so the seed of our emotional reaction is already there. This is what makes expectations and their pending or current reactions good candidates for the SEE Technique.

Being able to remember the future without attachment to the specifics of its timing, allows us to remain fully present in Pure Awareness so that we can respond to the needs of each moment with the fullness of our Being. What a great way to live. By cultivating this way of being by practicing the Pure Awareness Techniques, your life will rapidly become more the expression of perceiving intentions. Then you are available to step into the reality of the evolving intention as it naturally comes into being. This doesn't mean that you won't be doing anything. On the contrary! When you clearly distinguish between intention and expectation you simply stop absorbing yourself in useless notions about how you want the universe to organize things for you. Instead you are fully present to the WONDER of uncertainty, enjoying and delighting in the richness and adventure of each moment. The laws of nature flow through your body, mind and personality, sometimes with great dynamism. So don't be concerned that living from Pure Awareness is going to make you a couch potato. Far from it!

Cultivating the Distinction Between Thinking and Knowing

Now let's take a look at how to cultivate the ability to "know that you know", by using the Pure Awareness Techniques SANYAMA and WAIT.

The SANYAMA Technique – Silent Awareness Notices Your Answers Manifesting Automatically

"These days when I'm coaching someone and they don't know what to do I ask them to go into the GAP and have them drop their question into Awareness and simply wait for an answer. The answer usually surfaces as a Knowing, fully

formed and clear. Frequently, as an alternative to their asking the question, I'll drop a question into Awareness on their behalf. Sometimes, if we're both stuck, the best question is, "What is the optimum question to ask?" The thing I love about the SANYAMA Technique is that the person who is doing it is getting the answers from within themselves not from some outer reference or authority (such as me). It's great when the sense of what's right for them comes from within them! Then their Knowing guides them and it couldn't be more perfect or authentic than that. I just love the Pure Awareness Techniques!"

– Steve Straus

Checking Your Cosmic Email Inbox

The word SANYAMA is originally a Sanskrit word that was used by Yogi Patanjali in his treatise called the "Yoga Sutras." The SANYAMA practice starts with taking your awareness into Pure Awareness. You then allow your awareness to quietly have a thought and then surrender that thought into Pure Awareness. When done properly this can bring insights and clarity. It is after all your own awareness. It is where your knowing comes from. Even not getting a response is an answer. It means that it's not time to know yet. It means that your cosmic email inbox is empty. Practicing SANYAMA is essentially like learning how to check the inbox of your emails from the universe.

One of the attributes of Pure Awareness described in the ancient Vedic texts is the Sanskrit expression - Ritam Bhara Pragyam. This means the level of consciousness that knows only truth. It is after all our own awareness. This is the level of life from which we know things. It is where our knowing comes from and it is that with which we have all of our experiences.

When you surrender a thought into Pure Awareness when practicing SANYAMA, you will typically experience some kind of response. The response maybe an insight, a confirmation of something you already know, an idea, or more clarity about something. Whenever you are unsure about the response, then it may be that there is too much internal emotional or mental static or noise inside of you. Or it may be that it just isn't time to know yet. The nature of the universe is to be very efficient. It doesn't bother sending you an email until it is appropriate for you to know something. But sometimes it can be worthwhile to just settle down and check you cosmic inbox by practicing SANYAMA.

When you practice SANYAMA and drop a thought into Pure Awareness, it activates the laws of nature—the full power of the infinite potential that is latent in Pure Awareness. Practicing SANYAMA is a powerful way to bring yourself into alignment with these laws of nature. In SANYAMA, one does not command the laws of nature, but learns how to become one with them.

The Rediscovery of SANYAMA

I am delighted to acknowledge my dear friend and colleague Michael Stratford, who is the Director of the Core Dynamics Coach Training Program for Great Life Technologies, and who co-teaches this program with me, for rediscovering SANYAMA. I say this because while practicing the GAP Technique regularly, Michael discovered SANYAMA quite independently of knowing anything about Patanjali and the Yoga Sutras.

On New Year's Day, 2007 Michael was thinking about what was coming in the year ahead, and experiencing some uncertainty. While doing the GAP Technique that morning, he had the idea to go into

Pure Awareness and just ask the question, what, if anything, should he do to support bringing about the things he envisioned happening in the year ahead? Then he just relaxed into Pure Awareness and listened, and some surprising answers came to him that he felt he would never have thought of otherwise. Those answers gave him an entirely new direction for his business and coaching career. He suddenly got a level of clarity that allowed him to end his involvement with a coaching school he'd been working with for a long time, and instead focus his time and energy in new directions.

He was quite amazed by the experience, and immediately began using this technique with his coaching clients. When he guided his clients into SANYAMA, he found that they would typically get some kind of "knowing" or even very clear thoughts or ideas coming to them that they had never considered before. On one hand, they might discover that there is nothing at all to do; on the other hand, they might receive guidance about taking specific actions to facilitate bringing about a particular outcome.

When Michael first told me about this technique, he said, "Dropping a question into Pure Awareness is like putting a destination into a GPS (Global Positioning System) device. All of a sudden the path to where you want to go becomes perfectly clear." Based on this analogy, we developed a special version of SANYAMA that you will learn in the next section. It's called the GPS Technique. In this context GPS stands for "Gentle Provocation System."

Michael's insight about being in the GAP and then innocently floating a question into Pure Awareness and seeing what happens immediately reminded me of the practice of SANYAMA that I had learned years ago.

As you can probably tell by now I really like acronyms as they make it easy to remember the Pure Awareness Techniques. When I thought about the word SANYAMA I thought that just maybe Yogi Patanjali was playing a cosmic joke and actually remembered the future (in English) when he used this word to describe the process of dropping a question into Pure Awareness and then innocently observing whatever answer surfaced. The word makes such a perfect acronym for this process – Silent Awareness Notices Your Answers Manifesting Automatically!

Being Present to What Is

In order to allow yourself to let whatever comes from Pure Awareness to arise in your awareness during the practice of SANYAMA, you have to be willing to be present to "what is." This means not editing what comes to you. It also means not having any attachment to the outcome of your inquiry. The ability to be present to "what is" gets cultivated by the practice of the CORE and SEE Techniques. By practicing the CORE and the SEE Techniques often, you cultivate a confidence in your ability to handle any emotional experience that you might have. These two techniques develop a kind of emotional mastery within you. You become a kind of black belt master of handling feelings. This is not the mastery of suppression or making feelings go away. On the contrary, it is mastery of completing incomplete experiences with the CORE Technique. It is also mastering the ability to extract your awareness from being collapsed inside of and lost to your identifications, expectations, projections and reactions using the SEE Technique. Mastery of these techniques will set you apart from most of the people on this earth. The ones who don't have this kind of emotional mastery can't be present to "what is." They run from their feelings like a three year old. They are afraid of being overwhelmed by them. No wonder our prisons are 70% to 80% full of people who have committed drug or alcohol related crimes. These are people who are trying to self-medicate the best they can to escape the fear of being overwhelmed by their unresolved emotional pain and their unmet expectations. What they really need is education, so they can learn how to become competent at feeling. This is what gives us the ability to be present to whatever life brings us. The practice of the SANYAMA Technique also helps you to be present to "what is," present to the WONDER of uncertainty.

Remembering to Use the SANYAMA Technique

The Pure Awareness Techniques are of course only useful to you if you actually do them. In order to remember to practice SANYAMA some people use it as a regular practice in the morning right after doing the GAP and AGAPE. When you are saturated in Pure Awareness is a great time to practice SANYAMA. It is also great to practice SANYAMA any time you would like to get insight into something. Whatever it is that you would like more clarity about, just drop your question into Pure Awareness and see what happens. Remember that it has to be done without attachment to any outcome. You are not the one who determines if there are any emails in your cosmic inbox or not. All you're responsible for is checking it from time to time. You can't force Pure Awareness to give you an answer and you can't force the universe to send you an email. Also remember that no answer is an answer. It means that it's just not time to know yet. To know, when it is not time to know, would violate the law of least effort. So just check again later. This is a great way to get clarity and to know that you know.

How Practicing the SANYAMA Technique Impacts Your Life

Practicing SANYAMA changes your relationship with yourself and the universe. You really start to get the distinction between thinking and knowing, and you cultivate a willingness to only make decisions from clarity. You learn that you are not the author of actions - you perceive intentions rather than create them. This is a powerful contributor to the dismantling of the illusion of being your ego. The practice of SANYAMA also has the effect of aligning you with the law of least effort. It helps you get into "the Zone" in everything that you do. You begin to drop your habit of straining to make things happen the way you think they should. Of course this technique works in synergy with the other Pure Awareness Techniques. Use it to find out if it's time to know yet. It's a great practice. Enjoy it!

The WAIT Technique - Waiting Accesses Intuitive Truth

It was in January 2009 when I gained a profound insight that my Higher Self does have amazing Inner Wisdom.

I used to be late for appointments, which I did not understand as I was regarded as a person of responsibility. People know me as a well-seasoned professional coach with passion and a big heart. Obviously, being late did not seem to live up to the expectations of others or myself. Strangely enough, I was very punctual and even very early to many other appointments.

One day, I asked Tom why I so frequently cause myself to be late, and he asked me what I would get from being late. It was "freedom" that I came up with as an answer, as I did not want to feel "obligated" to do things. Tom asked me another question. Was I making these appointments because they were things that I wanted to do, or because I felt I "should" do them. I had never really thought of that before. As I did think about it, I realized that the appointments that I was late to were in fact ones that I really didn't want to be going to.

Tom explained that when I make a decision out of a sense of obligation, that it is a conditioned response. It isn't my authentic Self deciding, but my conditioned self that is making the decision that I later regret. I was being late to appointments as a kind of rebellion, a way of showing that I resented having to be there, and was not being true to myself. My Higher Self kept sending me signals that those commitments would not make me genuinely happy and I was not listening!

Tom gently guided me in how to use the WAIT Technique. He said, "Sharon, whenever you are asked to do something and you are not sure if you want to do it, wait for clarity. Buy time. Say, I'll have to check my schedule and will get back to you later. This way, you can wait and feel whether or not you really want to do that thing, or if it is more from a sense of obligation or duty."

So I followed his advice. Two wonderful things have happened. First, I now only make commitments out of love, not out of a sense of obligation. This brings me joy. And second, because of that, I am never late anymore. On the contrary, I'm usually early to appointments and my life is filled with joy!

Now I use the WAIT Technique to allow me to get the clarity to be true to myself about all kinds of things which leads me to be fully present each moment.

Life is wonderful!

– Sharon Yoon-kyung Noh

The WAIT Technique goes against the grain of a lot of our societal conditioning. We are all conditioned to be impulsive and reactive.

"Just do it!" is an all too common mantra. Being impulsive and reactive are expressions of our learned conditioned responses. They are not expressions of Pure Awareness. Albeit there are times when it is essential to act quickly, but acting quickly is distinctively different from being impulsive. Most people are unaware that of this distinction.

How to Do the WAIT Technique

In theory the WAIT Technique is pretty simple. You just... wait. But what do you wait for? How long do you wait? How do you know when you have waited long enough? The answer is that you wait for clarity that comes from Pure Awareness. The trick is really getting what that clarity means. Our normal decision making process is controlled by our thoughts and our emotions. We aren't even making our own decisions. Our conditioned responses are deciding for us. We are programmed to react, not to decide.

In Human Software Engineering we distinguish between two kinds of thoughts; natural intentions and conditioned responses.

By natural intentions, I mean the kind of intention that gets effortlessly manifested without you having to lift a finger. Sometimes you might be called upon to take action but your action has the same quality of effortlessness as the kind that makes the grass grow or the clouds blow by. It's that being totally "in the zone" kind of feeling, a sense of frictionless flow.

On the other hand, conditioned responses are learned behaviors. They are not effortless though we may have become quite competent at doing these conditioned behaviors. It becomes difficult to distinguish between effortless, and simply well conditioned. Living with conditioned responses may give the appearance of being effortless, even though they are far from it. Conditioned responses tend to be more like trying to force things to be the way that we expect them to be, or trying to get other people to do things our way, or chasing after something because we are longing to get a sense of fulfillment from attaining it. All of these kinds of decisions and the ensuing actions are coming from thoughts that are generated out of stories about what we "think" should happen.

Everyone has the ability to KNOW what is right and correct for them, but this is typically covered up by layers of conditioning and emotionally reactive habits. Think of impulsive purchases that you have made that you later regretted making. Getting into relationships that your intuition told you not to touch with a ten foot pole typically results in misery and suffering. Making impulsive decisions about career or money or health issues can be disastrous.

The ability to KNOW what is right and correct for you is very simple, but like all of the Pure Awareness Techniques it involves doing something that is the opposite of what we have been conditioned to do. That is to wait for clarity. Waiting for clarity means to not make decisions impulsively or emotionally. The basic guideline is: if your decision feels emotionally charged, don't make the decision, instead wait for clarity.

Waiting for clarity is not a passive process. Not at all. Waiting is a time to gather more information, let circumstances develop a little bit more. And it's a time to practice the other Pure Awareness Techniques. Use the CORE Technique to fully feel any feelings that the potential decision is bringing up. You can use the SANYAMA

Technique to check in with your knowing and see what kind of guidance you get, even if you find your cosmic email inbox empty, which basically means... wait some more.

Like all of the Pure Awareness Techniques you have to actually practice the technique in order to get the hang of it. This Pure Awareness Technique is a little different as there are no instructional audio files to listen to and no script to have someone read to you. Instead what is needed is to install an audio recording inside of yourself that repeats – Wait for clarity, Wait for clarity.

What does clarity look like? What does it feel like? Maybe it would help to describe what it is not. It's not emotional. It's not pressured for time. It's not concerned about missing out on some opportunity. It doesn't have anything to do with what anyone else thinks or feels about it or about you.

It is a calm, quiet inner knowing that something is either right for you or it's not. It is being true to yourself. Waiting for clarity allows you to align with a place within, where you are not reacting to outer demands. You can then take action based on confidently knowing what is right for you.

Many people have a deep seated habit of acting on their impulses while they are still caught up in non-clarity. Non-clarity has a feeling of pressure about it; or a feeling of confusion, or frustration, or fear, or a vague discomfort. These feelings may in fact be the vary barriers that block clarity in the first place. You can use the CORE Technique to feel into these feelings and complete them. Feeling into the core of the energy of these feelings, and completing the experience of that energy, brings you to a state of being in which you are no longer in the grip of the feeling. When this happens you will experience quietness, a sense of expansion, a sense of wholeness. Clarity comes from this place. This is Pure Awareness – the source of all clarity.

So when you experience clarity it has a quality of calmness, peacefulness, and a deep certainty that doesn't even need intellectual understanding. You simply KNOW. This is the only real basis for making any kind of important decision about your life. The experience of what your KNOWING feels like may be different than the way someone else will experience it. What will be valuable is to cultivate personal familiarity with what KNOWING feels like within you. When you KNOW, there is no doubt, there is no uncertainty, no questioning. You simply know. This is clarity. This is what you wait for.

Each of us is here for a purpose. We all have our own rhythm and our own contributions to make according to the unique expression of life that is innately built into each one of us. If you are always impulsively responding to what you think you should do, or how to please someone else, or avoiding doing something because you are afraid of some potential consequences, you are going to be continuously experiencing frustration, anger, bitterness and disappointment.

So why not start to learn how to wait for clarity now. It's so much better to align yourself with nature's principle of least action than it is to struggle to make things happen. Allow yourself the pleasure of trying this out. The next time you are about to make a decision, wait for inner clarity and see what happens. You will be thankful and energized that you did. When you begin experiencing the magic that comes from waiting you'll be a convert.

When to Use the WAIT Technique

- When someone is pressuring you to make a decision to buy something or make a promise or commitment of some kind.

- Whenever you are making big decisions like who to marry, where to live, what job to take, whether or not to start a new business, etc.

- Anytime you have doubts.

- Anytime a decision feels emotional.

- While waiting, fully feel whatever there is to be experienced. Use the CORE Technique or the SEE Technique if needed.

Are We There Yet?

A barrier to success when using the WAIT Technique is impatience. We are impatient when we have expectations that are not being fulfilled. The problem is not with the natural timing of what we are experiencing, it is that we are trying to force or dictate our ego's timetable for the fulfillment of our desire onto life, the universe, and the laws of nature. It's as if we are saying, OK God, Let thy will be done – but on my timetable, not yours!

Just the question, "How long do I have to wait," is a clear indication that there is an expectation. It indicates a sense of conflict between the way that we expect life to show up verses the way that it is.

We all know what it's like to have kids sitting in the back seat of the car asking over and over, "Are we there yet?" When you wait for clarity you don't have to ask anyone else what's happening. You are so present to the reality of the moment that you know what's happening. You don't have to ask someone else to make decisions for you or tell you what to do. You know when you are clear about something. If you notice being caught up in a wave of emotion about something that will be your indication to wait longer. You have a certainty about your knowing that doesn't need to be explained. Or you have a certainty of knowing that it isn't time to know yet and you are completely OK with that. Overcoming impatience so that you develop a state in which you are comfortable with whatever life presents to you in each moment, typically involves using the SEE Technique as impatience implies having an expectation. If you feel impatient use the SEE Technique on the energy of the impatience and then you will be able to wait without discomfort.

Living in the Wonder of Uncertainty

When we have to wait for clarity we call this "living in the wonder of uncertainty." In order to live in the wonder of uncertainty we have to make the shift from living in the terror of uncertainty. Most people are afraid of the unknown. This fear is what causes people to become "control freaks." Whenever we try to control things it is because we are afraid that something might happen that we can't handle, or that something might cause us to become emotionally overwhelmed. This fear is the residue (or the "residodo" as my friend Barbara Dillinger would say!) of the Core Dynamic of *Resisting Feeling Things Fully*. It is the deeply engrained conditioned response to attempt to set things up so that they will be known and predictable.

Good luck! Things are not predicable or certain. Things are very uncertain. Uncertainty is only a problem if we are afraid that we won't be able to handle whatever shows up. Otherwise what advantage could there possibly be in making decisions from uncertainty? What advantage could there be in basing your decision on anything other than clarity? It doesn't make sense to be impulsive about anything, just because it is so habitual for the majority of the population to do that. The driving force behind impulsive decision making is the terror of uncertainty. Do you really want the terror of uncertainty to be the basis of your decisions and actions? Of course not! What if you used the CORE or the SEE Technique to resolve the fear of uncertainty so thoroughly that you didn't have it anymore? What if you made a shift from living in the terror of uncertainty to living in the wonder and delight of uncertainty?

I remember clearly when this shift happened for me. Without realizing it I had been living in a subtle fear of what might happen. I had a constant undercurrent of apprehension that something bad might occur that I wouldn't be able to handle. After practicing the CORE Technique for a few months I shifted from this constant undercurrent of fear about what might happen, to a delightful kind of inner peace. I found that I had the certainty to handle whatever I needed to handle or the clarity that it simply wasn't time to know yet. Wow! What an incredible, delightful shift that was!

People don't want to wait because if they wait, they will have to face their fears of uncertainty that they intuitively know will surface. So making the decision to wait for clarity is actually going cold turkey on your addiction to being impulsive. It is learning to avoid being impulsive as a means to escape your fears of uncertainty. Practicing the WAIT Technique is making a decision to start resolving your fear of uncertainty.

When you choose to wait for clarity before making decisions it is very important to realize that you will come face to face with your fears of uncertainty. It's valuable to be conscious that this is going to happen. Fortunately, the CORE Technique that you are about to learn and the SEE Technique you already know, provide you with the resources and skills to face and handle the terror of uncertainty. You too can make a permanent shift from terror to wonder and delight.

It is so wonderful to begin to enjoy uncertainty instead of fearing it. While you may still have fears of the unknown, the WAIT Technique will allow you to come face to face with them so that you can then use the CORE or SEE Techniques to fully and completely liberate yourself from these insidious fears. It takes a decision and a commitment to pull this off. This book is providing you with the tools to do this but you don't have to go it alone. If you want help making this shift, hire a Core Dynamics Coach to help you along the way. They have gone down this path themselves so they know the lay of the land. When you want to know how to get somewhere, ask someone who knows the territory to show you the way.

As with all of the Pure Awareness Techniques, you get better at doing the WAIT Technique with practice. There is no set answer to the question of how long to wait, but the fundamental answer is to wait until you have that quiet, calm inner knowing that something is right for you. Different people experience this kind of inner knowing in different ways. Getting there requires practicing the WAIT Technique.

Another set of insights about how to know what is right for you and how to make decisions that are perfectly aligned with how you operate in life is called Human Design. Human Design is highly synergistic with Human Software Engineering. Conveniently, my wife Lynda Stone is a leading world expert and teacher of the Human Design System. In Human Design you can see exactly how you were designed to operate from the moment you were born. This is unlike astrology or any of the other esoteric systems. Human Design provides you with an individualized picture of where to look for your knowing. It's another way to achieve more clarity in your life. This is immensely useful and valuable. Waiting allows you to begin to live in alignment with your own personal human design. It allows you to live a strategy that is consistent with who you are designed to be and to follow your inner guidance. You will no longer be driven by your conditioning or need others to form the basis for your decisions and actions. You can learn more about Human Design at Lynda's web site at www.humandesigncommunity.com.

Why do we call waiting for clarity a Pure Awareness Technique? Because we want all of our decisions and actions to come from Pure Awareness. When we are caught up in our conditioned thinking, our expectations, or our emotional reactions, we lose connection with Pure Awareness. Our decisions then have a faulty basis. Waiting allows us the time needed to reconnect with Pure Awareness. It allows us to come into alignment with Pure Awareness so that we become part of the effortless mechanics of nature that bring about the fulfillment of our purpose. Waiting gives us the opportunity to live in the wonder of uncertainty. The wonder of uncertainty is Pure Awareness. Use the WAIT Technique whenever you are not yet clear. It is a very important aspect of The Power Of How.

The Distinction Between Waiting and Procrastination

Waiting is not to be confused with procrastination. What's the difference? Procrastination is putting something off because something about it makes you uncomfortable. You may think that you are just being lazy or you are indulging yourself in something that you enjoy doing more than the thing you are procrastinating doing. But if you are uncomfortable about doing something use the CORE or the SEE Technique on the energy of the discomfort. Once it resolves, if that thing you need to do is clearly the right thing to do, now it will be easier to not procrastinate and go ahead and do it.

Waiting is certainly different than this. Waiting is the thing to do when you aren't clear and you don't know what to do. If you don't feel that you have the clarity then it's time to wait. If you are clear and the clarity is that it is time to act then go for it.

There is always a distinction between the circumstances and our reactions to them. If you are having a reaction in the form of procrastination then the optimal thing to do is to resolve the reaction using the appropriate Pure Awareness Technique and then you'll be able to be fully present to the needs of the moment. You may or may not still need to wait for clarity. If you have doubts, either wait longer or use the SANYAMA Technique.

Remembering to Use the WAIT Technique

Remembering to use the WAIT Technique can be a little bit tricky because we are so conditioned to be impulsive and reactive. You may not be making a clear distinction between spontaneity and impulsivity. Being clear about this distinction is an important key to being able to successfully use the WAIT Technique. There are two simple rules for properly using the WAIT Technique.

Rule #1 - When in doubt, WAIT

Rule #2 - If there is any emotional charge involved in making a decision, you haven't waited long enough yet (and you also need to use the CORE or SEE Technique!)

Waiting is truly a spiritual practice because so often the reason that you are not waiting is that if you did wait, you would have to face some pretty uncomfortable feelings. Some of us are addicted to our impulsivity, even though it perpetually causes us suffering.

So again there is a decision to make. It is the decision to get good at waiting. If you "get it" that waiting aligns you with the universal law of least effort which allows you to be perpetually "in the zone" then why would you not want to master the art of waiting? So I invite you to make a decision and a commitment to yourself that you will master the art of waiting for clarity. So often you will find that the thing that felt so urgent to do something about before just gets handled without you having to do anything.

How Using the WAIT Technique Impacts Your Life

- Waiting brings you into alignment with the law of least effort

- It gives you the opportunity to address impatience and resolve it

- It brings you face to face with anything that would be a barrier to getting clarity

- It teaches you to distinguish between spontaneity and impulsivity

- It allows you to act only from clarity

- It becomes the effortless natural way to function when operating naturally from Pure Awareness

Waiting for clarity, one of the greatest inventions since the wheel... of time.

Section 4 - How to Debug the Pain-Body and Restore Your Innate Capacity to Feel

Let's say, just as an example, that your lover unexpectedly left you for someone else. You are heartbroken and the pain of the loss and the feeling of betrayal have been lingering for months or years. Or perhaps years ago you had a traumatic experience of being molested, (in any form) and the pain of that experience is still with you. Or you just heard some bad news and you are gripped by the feeling of sadness and disappointment. Or someone important to you has just done something that makes you feel hurt and resentful. Perhaps someone close to you recently died, a lover or a parent or a child and you are still grieving long after a natural grieving period would be over.

When we have traumatic experiences we are typically overwhelmed by the intensity of the associated emotion. Most people are NOT skilled at dealing with their emotional traumas. This is due to the Core Dynamic of *Resisting Feeling Things Fully* and everyone has this Core Dynamic. As a result of our preverbal childhood conditioning we tend to resist feelings and not complete them. This leaves us with lots of unresolved emotional pain from the past. And we collect more and more of it throughout our life because the conditioning of this Core Dynamic is still there in us. This unresolved emotional pain lies dormant inside us as the unresolved energy of incomplete experiences. I believe this is what Eckhart Tolle refers to as the pain-body that you may have read about in his books.

I'm not sure that we actually have a "pain-body" per se. It probably seems so because we accumulate so much unresolved emotional pain due to the Core Dynamic of . It also may be because without the

CORE and SEE Techniques the accumulated unresolved emotional pain may seem like it could be a permanent part of our body. But once you complete and resolve all of this emotional pain of the past using these powerful techniques then your body is free of the accumulated pain. Then the notion that you have a "pain-body" doesn't really apply to you anymore.

The concept of having a pain-body may be a useful one when you have tons of emotional pain stored inside of you. But it may be even more useful to think of it not as something that is a part of you but as simply an accumulation of incomplete experiences and reactions to identifications and projections. The idea of having a pain-body has a subtle implication of being identified with the accumulated pain. Most people are identified with their emotional pain because they don't have the skills to resolve all that pain. If your only technique is to just feel the pain you are probably not going to become a big fan of that. Just feeling the pain without the skills of the CORE that allows you to complete the experience and SEE Techniques in which you go out into Pure Awareness and watch the emotional energy fade back into nothingness, without these skills, just feeling you pain in the normal, inefficient way isn't really much fun. In fact it can get discouraging because it can be very slow going. This slow approach to feeling one's unresolved emotional pain could easily lead to the notion that we have a "pain-body."

Once you have become skilled at doing the CORE and SEE Techniques you will feel very encouraged that the resolution of your accumulated emotional pain from the past and your skill of resolving your reactions and projections will allow you to rapidly free yourself from being identified with and being burdened by emotions. You will see them simply as incomplete experiences of the past that you know how to efficiently complete. Or if the emotion is a projection or reaction that these are just the side effects of illusory stories that you have inadvertently become lost. But now you know how to extract yourself from them so they no longer represent such a huge task. You are about to learn the CORE Technique. Anyone who is competent at using the CORE and the SEE Techniques will begin to feel that although emotional pain does occur in and around your body, it's not a part of you. And although you body can create the energy of emotion, pain is not a permanent part of you either. It's only a temporary condition that is there to bring you some kind of experiential wisdom. The development of the Pure Awareness Technique and the efficiency with which they allow for the resolution of emotional pain may be providing us with an upgrade to the idea that we have a pain-body.

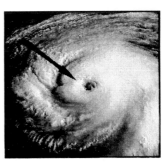

Our incomplete experiences are made of energy and the field of this energy is similar to the energy of a hurricane. The intensity of the energy is stronger nearer the center and weaker at the edges. Using the CORE Technique – an acronym for Center of Remaining Energy, allows you to experience the core of the most intense part of the energy of an incomplete emotional experience. It is like sky diving right into the center of the eye of the hurricane. There is a stillness in the middle. In fact, bringing your attention into the most intense part of the energy feels safer than any other part of the energy of the emotion, once you get there.

The CORE Technique is the quickest, most powerful and effective way of resolving incomplete experiences that I have found. When you put your awareness into the core of the most intense part of the energy of the incomplete experience, you allow yourself to complete the experience efficiently. When you stay out at the edges of the energy, or try to avoid it, you tend to hold onto it and it remains incomplete. It becomes an invisible barrier to clear decision making and a barrier to being clear about anything, including knowing what to do or who you really are. We have a tendency to avoid the intensity of the energy of a feeling by taking our awareness out towards the edges of it to avoid being overwhelmed by it.

Underutilization of Our Innate Capacity to Feel

There is a very good reason we have learned to avoid going to the center of the energy where the feeling is the most intense. We learned it when we were very young, typically when we were still pre-verbal. We all had emotionally overwhelming experiences when we were young and we made "feeling level decisions" to try to not feel things too intensely. It was our way to avoid being overwhelmed by emotions. Even today, we really hate the experience of being overwhelmed. The decision to resist feeling fully is still operating inside of us.

This decision to avoid feelings seems to be quite universal. This is a "feeling level decision" so there were no words available to us to create a description of this decision. This causes the conditioning of one of the Core Dynamics of Human Conditioning, *Resisting Feeling Things Fully*. Remember that each of the 12 Core Dynamics is the expression of a "feeling-level decision" that we made when we were very young. These decisions were not made with words. They are pre-verbal and pre-cognitive. When we grow up and acquire verbal and cognitive skills, we forget that we made these powerful feeling-level decisions. It seems to be universal to make a decision to do our best to avoid being emotionally overwhelmed, and we do this by shutting down our access to our own innate capacity to feel. See the Internet Resources section near the end of the book for more information and resources about the Core Dynamics.

The Tendency to Leave the Experience of Intense Feelings Incomplete

Unresolved emotional pain

As a result of this underutilization of our innate capacity to feel things fully, we tend to avoid completing intense emotional experiences. This causes us to accumulate "emotional baggage." We walk around with suitcases filled with these old unresolved, painful, intense feelings still held seething inside of us. Whenever life settles down for a few moments, there they are, pressing up to the surface, wanting to be felt and healed.

I have found that most people tend to be resigned to this state of avoiding feelings. They assume that it's just the way it is. This is a natural interpretation given the universal belief that everyone has very limited abilities to feel. But surprisingly, this is not actually true. It feels as if it's true, and it's hard to believe it could be otherwise (that's your conditioning speaking), but it's not true.

Remarkably, as we mature, we develop additional "spindle cells" in our brain that are necessary to process our emotions, even the painful and terrifying ones. But because by adulthood we have already been conditioned to avoid feeling fully, we still operate on our inner three-year-old's decision to avoid feeling things fully. This causes us to refrain from utilizing the natural innate capacities for feeling that are available to us as adults. We have the "hardware" to access our full spectrum of emotions, but our "software" for accessing and using this hardware is disabled.

This is like having a computer with terabytes of RAM and a powerful CPU but running on DOS. Even though there is lots of capacity, the operating system can't utilize it. What's needed is to upgrade the operating system to a more modern version that can use all of that latent capacity of the expanded hardware.

Underutilization of Our Innate Capacity to Feel

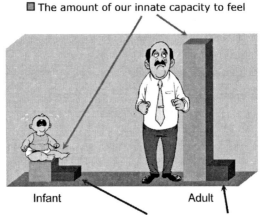

■ The amount of our innate capacity to feel

Infant   Adult

■ The amount of our capacity to feel that we access & use

Like that, our inner human software operating system is similar to a computer that needs to have its operating system upgraded. We need to upgrade from a state in which we unconsciously fear being overwhelmed to a state of being that allows us to access and use our underutilized capacity to feel. The way to upgrade your emotional operating system is to learn the CORE Technique. This will allow you to learn how to complete the energy of emotions in your body without the fear of being overwhelmed by them.

How Emotions Are Created

The field of Quantum Mechanics has shed some fascinating light on the nature of existence and our roles as creators. As explained earlier in the book, it is of course now common knowledge that all matter is made out of molecules. These molecules are in turn made of atoms that are in turn made of subatomic particles. Physics explains that the subatomic particles are made up of waves of energy. All different kinds of tangible physical things you can see and touch like cars, coffee cups, cell phones etc., plus the intangible things you experience; sounds, smells, tastes, are made out of waves of energy. In addition, all the things that seem even less tangible like thoughts, feelings, intuitions, perceptions, etc., are also made of waves of energy. What distinguishes whether that energy manifests as a coffee cup, a dog barking, or a stressful reaction appears to be the frequency and density of the patterns of their waves of energy.

There are countless studies documenting the electromagnetic properties of human beings. Our bodies, thoughts and feelings collectively create a unique electromagnetic human biofield that emanates from us. Recounting this research here is not necessary as this has already been brilliantly done by other authors including an excellent compilation by Dawson Church in his recent book, The Genie in Your Genes.[2] In addition, there are technologies such as Electroencephalographs (EEGs) that can measure the energy of our brain waves and Electrocardiographs that can measure the energy patterns of our heart, so this information is readily understood.

---

2   The Genie in Your Genes, Epigenetic Medicine and the New Biology of Intention - by Dawson Church

Scientific Research on Emotions and the Brain

New brain scanning devices have allowed scientists to discover that certain cells in the brain are responsible for processing emotional experiences. Experiments were 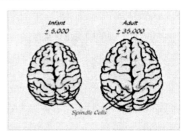 conducted whereby emotional stimuli were given to subjects while they were inside of a brain scanner. This allowed researchers to see which cells became activated by emotions. These brain cells are called "spindle cells." The scanners showed increased blood flow to these cells during the emotional stimuli. These recent findings have now made brain researchers confident that spindle cells are involved with the processing of emotional information.[3]

In addition, it was discovered that there are relatively few spindle cells in our brain during infancy. Thus, we don't have a great deal of capacity to feel and process our emotions because we don't have the "physical hardware" to do it when are very young. No wonder we get emotionally overwhelmed so easily! Between infancy and adulthood there is an apparent about a seven-fold increase in the number of spindle cells in the brain, and thus a substantial increase in our capacity to experience a wider range of emotions. So, it appears that as we grow, our bodies and brains acquire more "hardware" for processing feelings. However, due to our conditioning of *Resisting Feeling Things Fully*, this increased capacity tends to be grossly under utilized.

Remarkably, as we mature, we acquire the spindle cells necessary to

---

3   Humanity? Maybe It's in the Wiring, by Sandra Blakeslee, New York Times, December 9, 2003

process our emotions, even the very painful ones. But we are running on a three-year-old's decision to avoid feeling things fully, so we are not able to access our natural innate capacities for feeling that we already have. We do have "the hardware" to access the full spectrum of emotions that we were inherently designed to experience, but our software for accessing and using this hardware is disabled. We have a "bug" in our inner human software that has disabled our access to our own natural capacity to feel. We put a lid on it years ago when things just seemed to be too much to handle. This is why it can feel terrifying to even think about approaching that mountain of unresolved feelings... yet it can be easily done. Now it is possible to be free of them completely.

EEG Confirmation of the CORE Technique

In January of 2007 I gave a presentation about the work we are doing in Human Software Engineering with debugging ADD/ADHD at a neurofeedback conference in Palm Springs, CA called "The Winter Brain Meeting." During the conference I had the opportunity to test a new form of EEG monitoring equipment that allowed me to see the brain wave indications of the deep emotional releases people experience using the CORE Technique and other Pure Awareness Techniques that produce inner calm.

Great Life Technologies had a booth at the conference and I was mainly there to share our recent successes with debugging one of the major underlying causes of ADD and ADHD using new Human Software Engineering techniques and technologies. I gave a presentation about our work with this new approach. I also had the opportunity to give numerous demonstrations. People were fascinated, and many practitioners, heads of large clinics, and neurofeedback device manufacturers became very interested in our new techniques.

I began to explain the Core Dynamics of Human Conditioning to a woman at the conference who was fascinated with our work and wanted to know more. As we talked, she shared that the past year had been difficult for her, and that she was feeling stressed and very anxious as a result. She was a mid-level executive at a large company, and had been considering a change of career. She had never experienced anxiety before this period, which in itself was probably contributing greatly to her anxiety.

I helped her to identify where she was holding the energy of all of her stress in her body. It turned out to be in her solar plexus, which was very interesting. In the Eastern spiritual traditions, the site of the 3rd chakra is the solar plexus. It is sometimes called "The Power Chakra" and is associated with will power, vitality, and personal power. According to Eastern tradition, when people are out of balance in this chakra, they will often experience feelings of powerlessness: fear of taking risks, fear of confronting people or issues, fear of taking charge. In other words, they are stuck dancing at the outer edges of fear, and they commonly experience what we call "anxiety."

Using one of the advanced Core Dynamics coaching techniques, I debugged her inner human software for the Core Dynamic *Resisting Feeling Things Fully*, and I explained the nature of the kind of pre-verbal, pre-cognitive conditioning that produces our inner resistance to self-healing this kind of stress. I was just starting to teach her the CORE Technique and thought to ask her if she'd like to do this while using the new iCAP EEG monitoring device. This might allow us to see the effect of the technique on her brain waves. She said she would like to try this, so we went to the iCAP booth that was right next to the Great Life Technologies booth and asked if we could use it. The iCAP folks were as interested as I was to see what would happen.

As I guided her into the CORE of the feeling, I got to watch what was happening with the EEG on the laptop screen. With the iCAP system, a drop in the indicator line means that there is a release of stress and/or emotional energy occurring. As I guided her through the CORE Technique instructions, the indicator line begin to drop a few times. At a certain point, about three and a half minutes into the session, and after a short instruction about allowing herself to go right into the center of the most intense part of the energy of the feeling, there was a dramatic drop in the EEG indicator line.

Right at that moment, one of the founders of the iCAP company who was sitting nearby happened to look over. When he saw what was happening on the monitor his eyes widened and his jaw dropped open! He waited for a few moments, because he could see that she was in the middle of a deep release. He then said quietly (but with a strong enthusiasm in his voice), "Wow, your stuff really works! Getting below 300 is really extraordinary!" (In fact, the reading from the EEG had gone down into the 270's range during that big drop.)

The graph below shows what it looked like on the screen (with my notations added). There are two overlapping traces, one for the signal from the first 2 ½ minutes of the exercise and one that shows the activity of the second 2 ½ minutes. (On the computer screen they are different colors. As we are using black and white for the graphics in this book I've made one trace a dashed line and the other one solid.) She was starting to get the hang of it toward the end of the dashed line, then even more during the first 30 seconds of the solid line. At about 45 seconds into the solid line portion of the session, she completed the experience of the energy of the big knot of stress that she had been holding onto. Later she said that it was the cumulative stress of the entire past year and that she felt transformed during these few minutes. It is common for the EEG line to come back up after a release like this. The iCAP folks explained that the more such deep releases someone has the more their overall average emotional excitation level stabilizes at a lower reading over time. They can track and measure this type of progress from session to session. That of course doesn't show in just one session. A lower overall average level in a given session is apparently a common result as people resolve more and more of their deep inner stresses and is a good indication of their progress.

EEG Brain Scan During a Session Using the CORE Technique

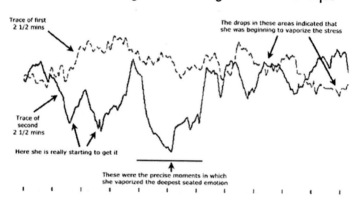

Trace of first 2 1/2 mins

The drops in these areas indicated that she was beginning to vaporize the stress

Trace of second 2 1/2 mins

Here she is really starting to get it

These were the precise moments in which she vaporized the deepest seated emotion

It was great to meet the people from iCAP and learn about their new EEG technology. It's a unique new form of EEG monitoring that is specifically designed to pick up and display brain wave patterns that indicate deep emotional releases. Best of all, it's very user friendly—it's completely wireless, and it doesn't require moisture for the sensor that picks up the brain waves. The small sensing unit is mounted in a simple elastic headband and sends a wireless signal to a small USB receiving device that brings the data into a very simple interface on your computer. The software allows you to witness in real time the direct effect of doing techniques that release emotions and create a deep state of relaxation. In addition to monitoring the emotional releases that occur in the moment, it can track your progress in cleaning out your emotional baggage over time. I am happy to endorse this great new product. You can read more about the iCAP EEG system in the articles section of our website at: www.greatlifetechnologies.com.

The CORE Technique – Center of Remaining Energy

"The Year 2000 was not an easy one for me. This was a year when I was really scared and almost crushed by the death of a very close friend who had inoperable brain cancer. That same week two of my other friends were diagnosed with breast cancer. The death and the two additional friends being diagnosed with cancer was more then I could handle. These devastating experiences triggered unresolved feelings of grief and a fear of death I had been storing for years after I witnessed both of my grandfathers pass away. I also manifested an odd tumor like mass in my own body. After surgery, I began frantically looking for solutions to both my health and emotional issues. This search became the main focus of my life.

In 2003 at the Future of Coaching Conference I met Tom Stone and a few months later I was enrolled in his educational program. While participating at his 12 Core Dynamics of Common Problems seminar I told him my story. Tom saw the depth of my grief and offered to lead me through the CORE technique. As I felt into the core of this energy, I was able to enter the deepest part of my being that was holding the trauma related to the fear of death. In just a few minutes I stopped crying and felt waves of relief. As I went deeper and deeper into the Core of my despair and feelings of guilt for not being able to save my friend's life, I found that it was possible to be with this energy without being overwhelmed by it.

This experience was a major turning point in my life. Not only was I able to release the old grief that I had been carrying for three years, I could now remember my friend with love, not with sorrow. I am now able to hold the space for others to experience the Core of their feelings instead of falling apart or crying with them as I used to do. This experience has given me the freedom to access my true core in any interaction or situation, and be able to stay 100% present to the experience no matter how intense it gets.

Hundreds of my clients have experienced the same results with The CORE Technique and the other Pure Awareness techniques developed by Tom Stone. I am so very grateful for having met Tom, and to make conscious shifts in my life inspired and supported by his mentoring, technologies and techniques. Love and deepest gratitude."

– Svetlana Pritzker

Resolving the Pain of the Past

Would you like a way out of the pain of the past? If so, I have news for you. The way out turns out to be... IN. Before I go too far in trying to explain something that you haven't yet experienced, I would like you to again go to our website and listen to some examples of people being guiding through the CORE Technique. Then I'll give you a step-by-step description of how to do it.

You can listen to the audio recordings of examples of the CORE Technique at

www.thepowerofhow.com/CORE.html

Welcome back.

Now that you've heard examples of people being guided through the CORE technique you can learn how to do it yourself. I recommend that you find a practice partner and go through the exercise with one of you guiding the other. Then switch roles so that you both get a chance to experience the process. Practicing the CORE Technique with someone's guidance the first few times usually makes it easier to learn than by simply doing it yourself.

In order to learn the Core Technique you have to be able to find the sensation of an unresolved emotion that is held in your body. We all know what it feels like to be angry, afraid or sad. With anger there is a raging energy that courses through us. We may feel it in our throat or our belly. It could be found anywhere. With sadness or fear it is often in our chest. Sometimes there are layers to an incomplete emotional experience; one stacked on top of the other. As you dive down into the core of the energy, a layer of it may seem to be gone but there may be another layer of emotional energy underneath the first one. If you find that this is so, you will want to find the core of the new layer and dive down into it. Sometimes there can be several layers, each with a different quality of feeling.

The first time I used the CORE Technique I experienced several layers of emotional energy, one seemingly on top of the other. I experienced the first layer as anger. When I had felt into the core of the anger so thoroughly that there wasn't any anger left, I found a feeling of hurt under where the anger had been. Again I felt down into the energy of the feeling of hurt until there was nothing left to feel. Under that there was sadness and then a feeling of being alone and isolated. When I felt into the most intense part of each of these layers of unresolved feelings I finally got to the bottom, and there was nothing left to feel. The experience was like the clouds burning off in the morning sun. Everything felt open and expanded. It was a clear experience of Pure Awareness. So if there are layers of feelings stacked one on top of the other, just find the center of each one and feel down into them until there is nothing left to feel.

Sometimes the layers of an incomplete emotional experience get stored in several different places on your "internal hard drive" in your body. You may find that when the energy of one of them seems to be fading away, the sensation and presence of another layer of energy will emerge in another part of your body. Whether there are several layers and locations or just one, when you feel your way down into the core of the most intense part of the energy of the sensation you will eventually find... "no-thing."

The nothing that you become aware of is the background of silence in which all of your experiences occur. The layer or layers of energy are simply incomplete experiences masking the experience of this background of silence. Each energy or layer of energy that you resolve with the CORE Technique is the remaining energy of your initial reaction, the experience that was not completed at the time of the reaction. When you efficiently complete the experience of the reaction there is often a sense of the energy diminishing and then dissipating. This happens as you get back to the source of the energy where the reaction was created in the first place. This source of the energy is Pure Awareness. Once you have experienced Pure Awareness using any of the Pure Awareness Techniques you will begin to recognize it when accessing it via another Pure Awareness Technique. So the Pure Awareness you experience during the CORE Technique is the same Pure Awareness, the same background of silence that you experience during the GAP or the SEE Techniques.

This nothingness from which the energy of the reaction was created has many of the characteristics attributed to the "Unified Field," as described in quantum physics. It is postulated that when you complete the experience of the energy of the reaction that you have been holding in your body, and you experience the nothingness of the background of silence, you may be directly experiencing the quantum field from which the energy of the experience had manifested.

Mastering this ability to access the state of Pure Awareness using the CORE Technique is a great skill that allows you to quickly come out of the limiting influence of the previously incomplete experience. It is the quickest way known to come out of the grip of an emotion and to complete the experience of the emotional energy.

Getting Ready to Start the CORE Technique

Find an emotional charge that is easy for you to feel in your body. A recent upset, a disappointment, a resentment, something that you're still a bit upset about, or something that you feel incomplete about, or traumatized about, or something you regret from the past. How about a former lover you still feel some heartbreak over, or a co-worker or family member you can't stand, or that feeling of rejection that you got when you asked that cute redhead down the hall out on a date and she turned you down. Find anything that has a residual charge to it, a feeling of discomfort and now think about it for a moment. By thinking about the story of the upset you intensify the emotional charge and the energy will be very identifiable. Once you can feel the charge somewhere in your body you can begin learning the CORE Technique.

You have to have something that you can feel in your body in order to learn this. If you can't feel anything then there is a provocation in the next paragraph that will likely get you in touch with a feeling in your body. If you can already feel the energy of an unresolved emotion you don't need this. But for now, if you can identify the sensation of—or the energy of—an emotion in your body, you can start with that. If so you can skip the next paragraph.

Provocation to get access to the energy of emotion in your body

This is only for people who are having difficulty feeling the energy of an emotion in your body. If you are having trouble feeling an emotional energy in your body it will probably work to think of someone you really love and then imagine for just a moment that you could never see them again. This will very likely get you in touch with the energy of the feeling of loss that is pretty universal. You'll probably feel it in your chest or belly. Once you can feel that energy in your body you are ready to do the CORE Technique to resolve it.

How to Do the CORE Technique

Have your practice partner read the following instructions to you while you sit comfortably with your eyes closed.

If you don't have a practice partner and/or you would like some professional help in learning the CORE Technique we have a large team of highly trained Core Dynamics Coaches who can guide you to do this over the phone or in person. You can visit www.thepowerofhow.com and get connected with a Core Dynamics Coach. Receiving guidance in how to do the CORE Technique is easily done over the phone by these skilled coaches. So you don't need to meet a coach in person to benefit.

If you do have a practice partner, have them read the following instructions to you. Note that the reader's script is in quotes. The text in italics is instructional for the reader and is to be read silently.

After you have identified an issue that has a remaining emotional charge to it you are ready to start.

—start here:

"Please close your eyes."

Wait for a few moments, then say.

"Notice that the sensation of the incomplete experience has an energy to it."

Wait for a few moments, then say.

"If you allow yourself to, you will notice that you can experience this energy somewhere in your body...

pause

in your throat, chest, solar plexus, belly... somewhere."

Wait for a few moments, then say -

"Where in your body do you feel the sensation of the energy of this incomplete experience?"

[They will say or gesture to an area in the chest or stomach or throat or somewhere. Then say -

"If you allow yourself to, you can sense in that field of energy, that there is an area where it is more intense than it is elsewhere. Can you sense that?"

They will typically acknowledge this with a nod or a yes. If not you can tell them to just allow themselves to feel the field of the energy for a little while and see if after a time they notice that there is an area that is more intense than elsewhere. In a short time they will tend to say yes. If not, you may have to use the guidelines for one of the variations of the CORE Technique that are explained later in this chapter. Assuming that they do acknowledge sensing an area in the field of the energy that is more intense than say -

"Now allow yourself to let your awareness go right into the center of the most intense part of the energy of the sensation."

Pause

"Can you do that?"

Pause – wait for acknowledgment

"Okay, go ahead and continue."

Now... WAIT, until you have a sense that it's appropriate to speak again. This will range from less than a minute to a minute or two or even more. Then say -

"Usually what happens is one of three things. Sometimes the sensation will become more intense at first as you haven't been allowing yourself to feel it fully. Sometimes it will seem to stay the same for a time. And sometimes it may start to fade away or soften. Is one of these things happening?"

Typically they will nod or say yes. If they don't volunteer anything you can ask –

"Which one of these are you experiencing?"

There are three possible responses:

1. It's getting more intense

2. It seems to be staying the same or

3. It seems to be fading away or becoming softer/less intense

For either 1 or 2 you can then say –

"OK, simply continue to allow your awareness to feel right into the center of the most intense part of the energy of the sensation."

Then give them some time to do that.

For a #3 response - it is fading away/becoming softer or less intense, say -

"Bring your awareness in closer to whatever is left of the sensation, again find the center of intensity of the remaining energy, and again allow yourself to feel down into it, just experiencing the essence of the energy."

"The idea is to feel down into the energy of the sensation so thoroughly that there is nothing left to feel."

Then give them some time to do this. Then check in again with them to see what is happening. You can say –

"How's it going?"

They may have had some visual experience or the energy they are sensing may have moved to a different place or they may have completed the experience and the energy will have dissipated, and there's nothing left. If they say anything other than what they found in there was nothing, you have to continue to guide them into the core of the energy of the experience.

"Is there any of the sensation of the energy left" or "Is there any charge left?"

If they say yes, then say -

"Okay, I'd like you to again place your awareness into the center of the most intense part of whatever is left of that energy. We're not looking for insights, just experiencing the energy of an incomplete experience. This is just the process of completing the experience of the energy that has been held in your body. I'd like you to allow yourself to experience it so thoroughly that there is nothing left to experience."

Continue with them in this way. In the vast majority of cases, the person will come out of the grip of the energy of the incomplete experience, and they'll say something like, "It's better" or "It's gone" or "there's nothing there."

Once they experience that there is nothing left and there is no more energy of the sensation you can now do what is called a provocation test. This is to make sure that they really fully experienced every bit of the energy of the incomplete emotional experience and there's truly nothing left of it. Say to them –

"Now that it appears to be gone we are going to check to see that it's really complete. So I'd like you to think about the original thing that was causing this sensation in you."

Give them a moment. Then say -

"Is there any charge still associated with the original experience? Is there any remaining charge to the feeling that was originally there?"

Typically, they'll say "No. It's gone." (Don't be surprised if they smile or look relieved.) Then you can say this –

"You are no longer limited by the presence of the energy of that incomplete emotional experience. Your body has been trying to get you to fully feel this energy and complete the experience that

was held there. Now it is complete and your body has stopped creating this energy. There was an experience of something there that your body needed you to get, not intellectually but experientially. From this place that you're in now, this place of nothingness, you have total freedom of choice...you're in a state of all possibilities.

They may have opened their eyes by now but if they haven't you can invite them to do that now.

This is the end of the guidelines for doing the CORE Technique.

When to Use the CORE Technique

Now that you have learned how you do the CORE Technique I want to address when to use it. You can use the Core Technique any time you feel like you are getting lost to the grip of an emotion. Sometimes a circumstance will trigger some incomplete experience from the past and you will feel an emotional charge. This is a perfect time to remember to use the CORE technique. Once you come out of the grip of the emotion, you are now in a state of Pure Awareness. You can make the best decisions for your life from this state—but not when you are in the grip of emotion. Use the CORE Technique every time you feel that your emotional reactions are getting the best of you. With practice you will never have to be the victim of your emotions ever again.

You can use the CORE Technique two different ways.

Use it to come out of the grip of emotion whenever you feel you are becoming overwhelmed, or just have some feeling that you would like to resolve.

You can use the CORE Technique in the context of Core Dynamics Coaching sessions. A trained Core Dynamics Coach asks questions to help you identify any "archived" incomplete emotional energy that may be causing a barrier to achieving the life you want. Core Dynamics Coaches skillfully inquire into the nature of what is happening and are able to get you in touch with anything that might be blocking you from operating from Pure Awareness. They will then carefully guide you through the use of the CORE Technique (or the other Pure Awareness Techniques as appropriate) to resolve the basis of your inner conflict and remove this self-sabotaging inner barrier from your life.

In both cases the CORE Technique is the same. You feel down into the center of the intensity of the energy of the feeling until you have felt it so completely that there is nothing left to feel.

A few words of additional guidance here may be helpful. Because we are deeply conditioned to go away from where the emotional energy is the most intense, we will have an automatic tendency to not use the CORE Technique. It takes going through the process a number of times until we have developed the new habit of using the CORE Technique instead of avoiding it and giving in to or avoiding our emotionally intense experiences.

This leads us to the next important point –

The Biggest Mistake You Can Make

The biggest mistake you can make with the CORE Technique is also caused by our early childhood conditioning. Sometimes, especially when people are first learning how to do the CORE Technique, they will feel into the feeling for a while and the energy will lessen. Instead of completing the experience they will open their eyes and say, "It's better" feeling like they are finished with the exercise. However, we don't want to leave the experience incomplete. Better doesn't necessarily mean completed. The biggest mistake you can make with the CORE Technique is to NOT complete the experience of the energy that is being held there in your body. It is your conditioning— the Core Dynamic of *Resisting Feeling Things Fully* that causes you to want to go away from where the feeling is intense. It's a common experience that you feel like you want to stop and not continue under these circumstances. Therefore, it is very important to understand this dynamic and to keep feeling down into the center of the intensity of the sensation until there is nothing left to feel. These are the important words to remember –

Feel into the core of the energy of the feeling so thoroughly that there is nothing left to feel.

Doing the MapQuest Thing

Something that can help to insure that you do feel into the core of the energy until there is nothing left to feel is to do what we call the MapQuest thing. Everyone who uses the Internet knows about MapQuest. There are other similar mapping programs, however this was one of the first mapping web sites so it gives a familiar name to this idea.

When you are using MapQuest and you want to get a closer view, you "click in", meaning that you click the map and there is a "zooming-in" effect that lets you see a greater level of detail. It is like increasing the magnification using a telescope or a telephoto lens from an airplane or satellite.

When you are feeling into the core of a feeling and it starts to fade away, rather than succumbing to the tendency to call it a day, "click in closer" and bring your awareness in closer to whatever remains of the energy of the sensation in the body. Again, find the center of the remaining energy and continue to feel down into it. The idea is to keep clicking in closer and feeling into the core and clicking in closer and feeling into the core until there is nothing left to feel.

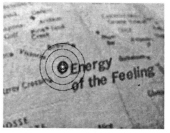

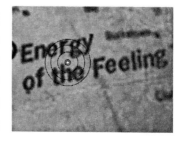

A related issue is the attitude that you hold regarding the emotions that are held in your body. Due to the conditioning of *Resisting Feeling Things Fully*, we can have a tendency to adopt an attitude of wanting to make the bad feelings go away! It's because of our fear of being overwhelmed by the feeling. We have a lifetime of perpetuating the childhood notion that we can't handle the feeling and are going to be overwhelmed by it. This can cause us to try to force the completion of the experience of the energy when doing the CORE Technique.

However this is counter productive. Forcing it will tend to cause straining and resistance and can get in the way of allowing yourself to fully complete the experience. So just know that doing the CORE Technique is not about making the feeling go away or getting rid of the feeling. Instead, have the idea that you are gaining the skill of completing incomplete experiences. It is the completion of the experience of the energy in the body that allows the body to stop creating that energy.

The body creates the energy of emotions. It is something quite natural to us, and essential to our survival. If we are standing on the railroad tracks and a train is coming toward us, thank goodness our body has the innate intelligence to create the emotion of fear that motivates us to get off the tracks. The same applies to walking up to the edge of a cliff. The fear that is generated in the body keeps us from going over the edge.

This means that when there is an incomplete emotional energy stored in the body, it's our body's way of telling us we have something to fully experience. The attitude of "getting rid of it" tends to cause us to stuff or repress the feeling. This is ignoring the body's innate intelligence. The body is trying to bring us a kind of experiential wisdom. This wisdom comes from allowing ourselves to complete the experience of the sensation that the body is bringing us. Therefore, it is important to shift your attitude from one of making it go away, to allowing yourself to complete the experience.

Laser Beam versus Flashlight Beam

Yet another related experience that can happen during the CORE Technique is that sometimes it may seem like it is taking a long time to complete the experience of the energy of the sensation or feeling. If this happens it may be an expression of some of the subtle influences of the Core Dynamic - *Resisting Feeling Things Fully*. Due to the tendency and habit of going away from where the energy of the sensation is the most intense, your awareness may tend to "spread out" and be more like a flashlight beam rather than focused like a laser beam. If your awareness is more like a flashlight beam then you won't tend to complete the experience of the energy of the feeling very quickly. Although we aren't in a rush when we're doing the CORE Technique, we do want to be efficient about completing the experience. This is why we go to the center of the intensity of the energy of the feeling. This is where we get to experience the real essence of the feeling, the most concentrated part of its energy. This allows us to complete the experience in the most efficient possible way.

When we use a laser like focus of our awareness when doing the CORE Technique, it can make the difference between taking just moments versus taking hours or days to complete the experience. You will find that you become more effective with practice. Each time you do the technique you'll get better at it. After doing the CORE Technique a couple of dozen times, you will discover that as you feel down into the energy of the feelings in a laser like way, the process will sometimes be completed in seconds. Decide to become a "black belt" master of using the CORE Technique. Developing this mastery will serve you very well throughout your entire life.

Subtle Variations of the CORE Technique

Now I would like to tell you about some of the different kinds of things that you may experience and give you some refinements and subtleties of the technique.

There is a wide range of possible experiences using the CORE Technique and as you continue to practice you may experience many of these variations. It may be useful to know the lay of land of your inner landscape of stored emotional energies so that you will not resist your natural experiences or be concerned about any of these things that may show up.

The Eye of the Hurricane

As explained earlier, sometimes as you feel down into the energy of the sensation or feeling in the body, it will seem as if there is a vortex, a kind of eye of a hurricane right in the center of the energy. If your experience is like this, let your awareness be like a laser beam going right down the center of the vortex. Keep following it down to the bottom of the vortex and it will open up into the experience of Pure Awareness.

What if I Feel Like Crying?

Sometimes you may feel like the energy is just too intense and you may feel inclined to be sucked into it or overwhelmed by it. You may feel like you are about to cry. There's nothing wrong with crying but it may not be the most efficient way to completely resolve the energy of the incomplete emotion that is held there. If you think about it for a moment, at what age did you learn to be overwhelmed by emotions and collapse into the feeling and cry? Pretty young, that's for sure! Allowing ourselves to collapse into crying and be overwhelmed by the energy of an emotion is a learned behavior from a time when your capacity to feel things was much less than it is now. You were very young and had a delicate nervous system that was easily overwhelmed. You may have developed the habit of crying at that time because it was all you could do.

Certainly there is some release from the emotion that happens from crying, but often there will still be residual energy that can be triggered again by certain circumstances. Crying then becomes yet another way to avoid feeling into the core of the energy. Crying doesn't typically complete the incomplete experience held in your body. It also doesn't typically bring you into the state of Pure Awareness.

Our aim is to resolve these incomplete experiences that are being held in the body so thoroughly and completely, that they are no longer barriers to our experiencing Pure Awareness all the time. As long as we continue to avoid feeling these incomplete feelings held in the body, they act as a kind of screen in between us and the continuous experience of Pure Awareness.

Therefore, you may find it more helpful to take your awareness inward to the center of the intensity of the incomplete emotional energy and feel down into it until the experience is totally complete. This will free you from any residual energy that the body is trying to get you to feel. The body is very tenacious. It will keep producing the same energy until you allow yourself to complete that experience. Once it is complete, then you are free of it forever.

It's like running anti-virus software on yourself. Once the virus is gone, it's gone and won't come back again unless you have another traumatic experience similar to the previous one that put it there. But there is very little likelihood of this happening because you are much bigger and stronger now, particularly now that you know how to do the CORE Technique. The CORE Technique helps to permanently resolve incomplete energies for two reasons

You will become increasingly able to stay present to intense experiences without being overwhelmed. Your experience will be that you can stay present to emotional intensity much more easily because you have been exercising your "feeling" capacity. When you fully experience things as they happen, your body doesn't have to "archive" the incomplete emotional energy and store it for later processing because it isn't incomplete!

Even if you do have another overwhelming experience that is similar to the one that you already completed using the CORE Technique, you have the CORE Technique which you can simply use to complete any new or similar incompletion that you may have in that moment.

Patterns of Energy that You May Not Recognize at First

Sometimes when there is something to feel into it may not at first be obvious that what you are feeling is a pattern of energy. This is especially true for things like feeling "empty" for example. Emptiness doesn't seem like it would be a feeling or a pattern of energy. So the trick to catching these patterns of energy that don't even seem like they could possibly be patterns of energy, and certainly don't seem like "feelings", is to use the very nature of what they do "feel" like as the way to get at them.

In other words, if you are feeling empty, you allow your awareness to go to the area that feels the MOST empty. This is a version of the most intense part of the energy of the feeling. There is a subtle but important difference between the "feeling of emptiness" and the experience of Pure Awareness. The feeling of emptiness has the implication that there is an expectation that something should be there. There is a feeling that there should be something there, and something is missing. Whereas in Pure Awareness, even though there is nothing there to experience in the form of an object, the sense of "no-thingness" feels alive. There is a sense of limitless potential, a feeling of pure possibility. Pure Awareness is the source of all of our experiences. Emptiness is the experience of feeling the lack of something. In Pure Awareness there is no sense of lack.

So if you feel "empty" then feel into the most intense part of the emptiness. This brings up another important point about the CORE Technique. There may be a tendency to begin to think that the feelings that come up and the experience of feeling into them is going to be the same as it was each time that you have done it before. Although often it may be similar, sometimes the quality of the experience of the energy will be different, in fact quite different, as in the case of "a feeling" of emptiness.

There may be other feelings that may surprise you because you would not characterize them as feelings. So it may be useful to simply think of them as any experience other than Pure Awareness. Once you have done the CORE Technique and the GAP Technique many times, you are going to be quite familiar with Pure Awareness. You'll be able to tell when something you are experiencing is NOT Pure Awareness. If something is bothering you, if it is making you uncomfortable, and especially if you don't want to feel it, that's the perfect indication that there is something that needs to be felt and completed.

Using the Core Technique to Resolve the Incompletions that Cause Worry, Anxiety, Nervousness and Depression

Another subtle variation of the CORE Technique is using it to resolve the underlying incompletions that cause worry, anxiety, nervousness, and depression. This is a wonderful application of the CORE Technique and you can use it immediately to dissolve any of these feelings regardless of how long you have had them.

The reality is that what we call nervousness, worry and anxiety are actually just the outer edges of the energy pattern of fear. We have developed a habit of taking our awareness out to the outer edges of a feeling of fear so that we aren't overwhelmed by the fear itself. The following is a practical variation of the CORE Technique for resolving the underlying fear in anything that you are worried, nervous or anxious about.

If you think about it, when things are disturbing, you can feel the energy of the worried or nervous or anxious feeling in your body.

These kinds of feelings tend to either be everywhere or they may have the feeling of surrounding your body and enveloping it. This experience is due to the conditioning of *Resisting Feeling Things Fully*.

So here's what you do. Allow yourself to feel the entire field of the energy that comprises the worry, nervousness or anxiety. Just allow yourself to be fully present and feel the whole of its energy. What will gradually happen is that you will start to notice that in the field of energy, there is an area where it is more concentrated, more condensed. It will usually tend to be toward the center of the body, somewhere in your chest or solar plexus or belly (but it could be anywhere). Once you notice it you can use the CORE Technique to allow your awareness to penetrate right down into the center of the most intense part of the energy of the feeling. You can continue using the rest of the CORE Technique in the normal way—making sure that you click in closer and feel into the Core of the energy of the feeling until there is nothing left to feel.

When it is all complete and there is nothing left to feel, open your eyes and think about the thing that was worrying you or making you feel nervous or anxious. Do you still feel that way? I'll bet not. If you do, go back and complete the experience of whatever is left of the energy of that feeling.

The same thing applies for depression. Depression is simply the outer edges of sadness. It may be a very painful sadness, so we are again habituated to going out to the outer edges of the sensation of the sadness in our body.

To resolve depression, start by allowing yourself to feel the entire field of the energy of the depression. You will gradually start to notice that there is a more condensed or concentrated area within the field of the energy of the depression. You will typically find it more towards the center of the body.

Once you are aware of the more condensed part of the field of the energy of the depression, allow your awareness to penetrate down into the center of the most intense part of the energy of the sensation. Using the CORE Technique, click in closer and closer and keep feeling into the center of the most intense part of the energy of the feeling until there is nothing left to feel. Scan the whole area inside of your body where the sadness energy was being held. Make sure that you have felt it so thoroughly that there is nothing left to feel.

Now see if you can provoke it and feel the depression. Try to recall the feeling of depression and see what happens. You will be amazed that it is simply gone. If you'd like more details about using the CORE Technique and some of the other Pure Awareness Techniques for resolving anxiety please see my book "Vaporize Your Anxiety without Drugs or Therapy" that you can find at www.VaporizeYourAnxiety.com.

Sometimes the worry, nervousness or anxiety are due to projecting possible negative outcomes onto the future. Likewise, sometimes the sadness or disappointment that is creating depression can be due to some major unmet expectation. When these are the causes of these feelings, then the SEE Technique will be more effective than the CORE Technique for resolving them. Start by allowing yourself to feel the entire field of the energy of the emotion and just notice how big it is. Go out to the outer edge of the energy of the emotion and notice the quietness out beyond the edge. Follow the rest of the guidelines for doing the SEE Technique and you will find the energy of the feeling fading away into nothingness. If you tried the CORE Technique and it doesn't seem to be resolving your worry, anxiety, nervousness or depression, use the SEE Technique and see what happens. Between the two techniques you will find that you can resolve any of these feelings easily.

A word about nervousness – Nervousness is typically a mixture of excitement and fear. The part of the energy of the emotion that you use the SEE or CORE Technique on is the fear component. Once the fear part of the feeling is gone you may still feel the excitement. Because the fear and excitement have usually been mixed together you may not at first be able to distinguish between excitement and nervousness. This is because the excitement part of nervousness is still there and you have associated it with the fear part of nervousness in the past. Allow yourself to enjoy the excitement and feel the absence of the fear. When you are successful with resolving the fear part of the nervousness using the SEE or CORE Technique you'll find that with just a little attention and practice you'll see that you will have shifted from nervous to excited. It's enjoyable to notice the difference.

Gatekeepers

Sometimes the energy of the feeling you're holding inside doesn't seem to get completed no matter how much you use the CORE Technique and feel into the heart of it. This happens because some emotions have been with us so long that they feel like they are a part of who we are. They aren't of course, but these feelings can be so compelling that when we attempt to feel into an emotion and complete it, there is another part of us that's afraid we will no longer know who we are.

It would be a mistake to underestimate the incredible power a fear like that can have over our lives. Inside ourselves we may feel, "Who will I be if that feeling I've been holding onto for all these years really does go away?" If we could articulate it we might say to ourselves, "If I complete the experience of this emotion, then it's going to feel like part of me won't be there anymore. I'll lose a part of myself that I am used to having around and that seems really frightening. I don't like having this emotional pain, but then again at least it's familiar. If it's gone I won't know who I am anymore."

When the energy won't resolve using the CORE Technique no matter how much we try, we call what is keeping us from resolving it a

"Gatekeeper." It's like having an armed guard standing in front of the door. It just won't let you in. Gatekeepers are usually the energy of the fear of letting go—in this case, letting go of something that has felt like it is a part of you for so long that you won't know who you are if it's gone. In the Core Dynamics model, our set of insights into the nature of pre-verbal conditioning, we call this the Core Dynamic of Resisting Change.

When you run into a Gatekeeper, it can feel like the CORE Technique is not working. When this happens there is a way to get to Pure Awareness through a "side door", and that's to use the SEE Technique that you already learned earlier in the book. When the CORE Technique isn't working, you can switch to the SEE Technique. You may also need to switch to the SEE Technique when you are stuck fearing that you will not know "who you are" if you completely resolve the energy you were feeling into. You will find that it is most effective to use the SEE Technique not on the original emotional energy but on the fear of not knowing who you will be if that energy was really completely gone. As you know, rather than going into the CORE of the energy of the feeling, the SEE Technique takes you in the opposite direction. It takes your attention out to the edges of the feeling. But instead of staying stuck in the outer edges of the feeling, you'll take your awareness just a little bit further. When you do this you access Pure Awareness—the silent background in which the experience of the emotion is occurring.

Once your resolve the fear of not knowing who you will be, you can then come back to the original emotional pain on which you were using the CORE Technique. Sometimes you will find that it is already gone. Other times it may still be there but now it will be easy to feel into and resolve it because the fear of letting it go and losing the sense of yourself that had been blocking the resolution of this energy inside of you for so long, is now resolved.

Toggle back and forth between the CORE Technique and the SEE Technique if you need to. This is a very potent combination and there doesn't seem to be any emotional residue or reaction that cannot be resolved using these two powerful Pure Awareness Techniques.

How Does the Energy of Unresolved Emotional Pain Impact Our Daily Lives?

One of Quantum Mechanics foundational principles is that everything is produced out of a field of pure potentiality, a limitless field of pure energy and information which has not yet become expressed in any physical form. The theory is that everything is created from this field of pure potential. This includes the experiences of our emotions. Our brain and body create the experience of emotion as a response to some outer stimulus. However, the emotion itself is a pattern of energy that we create within ourselves as an automatic reaction to a particular situation that is either pleasant or threatening. We use the term pattern of energy because different emotions have different vibrational patterns to them.[4,5] This is how we distinguish between fear, anger, sadness, joy, ecstasy, etc.

Is This a Form of Therapy?

I have been asked if the CORE Technique is a form of therapy. My response to this is that although it may have a wonderfully therapeutic effect, i.e. it can relieve deep seated traumas and emotional pain, it is actually just a "training", in how to access and effectively utilize our previously underutilized capacity to feel. Everyone has this innate

---

4   Power vs. Force: The Hidden Determinants of Human Behavior, by David R. Hawkins, MD, PhD
5   Institute of HeartMath, a non-profit research organization that investigates emotional energy and intuitive development

capability; we just haven't learned to use it.

This is similar to the development of the ability to read written words silently and understand their meaning. The ability to read written words that are formed out of combinations of individual letters is commonly attributed to the ancient Greeks, and apparently developed about 2,500 years ago. This was a major advancement and simplification over the former Egyptian method of using hieroglyphics or pictures to represent spoken words. It made it much easier for people to learn how to read. Apparently in the early days of reading, it was all done by saying the sounds of the letters and words out loud. For centuries most people had to read out loud in order to understand the meaning of words and sentences. The ability to read silently was unusual for most people and only became widely taught and practiced in the 20th century. To quote Robert Wilson, a historian on the teaching of reading:

"Oral reading was usual. St. Augustine, for instance, was perplexed by St. Ambrose's habit of silent reading (in Confessions). The importance placed on it can still be seen by observing the lip movement of some religious people when they are reading their scriptures. It was only after the invention of the printing press made mass production of books possible, that silent reading became usual, but the recognition and teaching of it as a special skill had to wait until the 20th century."[6]

Imagine the amazement of the people who could read out loud but not silently when someone started to be able to read words and know their meaning without speaking them out loud. It might have seemed to be a miracle! And yet, now we take silent reading for

---

6   Used by permission from an article entitled Teaching Reading—A History by Robert McCole Wilson found on the internet at http://www.zona-pellucida.com/wilson10.html#r3. Author's address: Robert McCole Wilson, (87 Cottonwood St.) Box 838, Lake Cowichan, B.C., V0R 2G0 Canada. Author's email: rmw@island.net

granted. Human being's had the capability to read silently all along, but didn't always appreciate that they had it or know how to utilize this natural capability.

We all have the innate capability to feel things fully and to do the CORE Technique. We seem to live at a time in human development that is similar to the time when we only knew how to read out loud. Our ability to access and use our innate ability to feel seems to be quite limited by our conditioning.

The development of the CORE Technique is somewhat analogous to the invention of the printing press. Everyone can now learn how to do the CORE Technique and enjoy the enormous advantages of being able to resolve the unresolved emotional pain of the past and live more and more from Pure Awareness.

So is this a form of therapy? I think not. It is a form of training, a form of education on how to use formerly under utilized parts of our natural abilities. Anyone who can feel can learn to overcome their conditioning of being resistant to feeling, and learn to use the CORE technique to clean up their inner emotional and energetic landscape.

Remembering to Use the CORE Technique

The most important aspect of the CORE Technique is remembering to use it. Once you have learned it, it's a bit like upgrading your inner human software. Now you have a new icon of inner human software sitting on your desktop. Just like with computer software, this new capability isn't going to do you much good unless you double click on it and use it!

The best way to remember to use this wonderful new tool is to make a decision that you are going to become really good at it and that you are going to use it every time you get caught in the grip of an emotion. After you have done it a couple of dozen times you will have probably overcome the reticence about feeling your feelings so fully. Once this has been overcome the use of the CORE Technique will simply become a normal part of your skill set, like reading silently is. You won't have to try hard to remember to use it because it will have become a natural part of your life. It will be right there and you will use it whenever the need arises.

How Using the Core Technique Impacts Your Life

There is a nice positive side effect of doing the CORE Technique many times. You will start to dismantle many of your life strategies of avoiding the possibility of being overwhelmed. You will gradually resolve your fears of that happening. This will allow you to start being more true to yourself, to start trusting and consistently acting on your intuition, to become much less or completely non-judgmental and to be able to be fully present to just about anything. What all of these things have in common is that they require the ability to feel fully. Gaining mastery with the CORE Technique will allow you to find your life growing and becoming enriched in extraordinary ways that you never imagined would be possible!

The GPS Technique – Gentle Provocation System

The Subtle Emotional Pain Vacuum Cleaner - A Special Use of SANYAMA

I used the GPS Technique on a pervasive feeling of being alone and lonely. I realized that I had this feeling all of my life. It took me about 45 minutes of doing the GPS before the loneliness feeling was completely cleared from every part of my body. Since then I can be alone without the feeling of being lonely. I feel so at home within myself.

Since then, when I get up in the morning I start my day by doing the GPS Technique. I make sure that if there was any residual stress from the day before or any unresolved issue from the past that was recently triggered, that I clean it up. I clean up all of the energy held in my body before I start my day. I love doing this. It's like taking an internal shower before I take my normal shower. I use GPS and the other Pure Awareness Techniques at other times, but this morning practice is precious to me.

– Adriana Bacelis

How to Access and Resolve Residual Subtle Emotional Pain

Sometimes there are patterns of energy held in the body that you can't seem to get access to for doing the CORE Technique. You may feel a sense of incompletion about something and know there is still some energy held in the body about a certain issue, but you just can't seem to locate or get to it by talking about it. The normal verbal provocation techniques of having you imagine the situation so that you can get in touch with the feeling just don't seem to be getting at it.

This is an opportunity to use the SANYAMA Technique in a special way that we call the GPS Technique. The GPS Technique gives you instant access to any patterns of energy still held in the body related to any specific issue, without having to imagine anything about the issue and without trying to visualize anything. It gives you access to any remaining energy of an incompletion. It starts by going into Pure Awareness using the GAP Technique just as you would usually begin the SANYAMA Technique. Then you drop your inquiry into Pure Awareness by asking to become aware of any remaining energy related to the particular incompletion that you would like to have fully resolved. In this case, you're asking not for ideas or insights, but simply to be made more aware of any incomplete energy that you might still be inadvertently holding in your body related to this issue.

Here's an example of using the GPS Technique with a client who had a very subtle fear of being vulnerable. Without being aware of it he was holding himself back from being even more successful in his life. The way that we discovered it was that he was teaching a course and he was finding that the students weren't responding and participating as much as he wanted. He was already quite familiar with the Core Dynamics, so rather than blaming the students, he took this as a cue that perhaps there was some subtle way in which this behavior of the students might be a reflection of something going on inside of him.

As he was sharing this experience with me we were able to identify that he had a subtle inner fear of being vulnerable or exposed, and we realized that this fear was being "mirrored" to him by his students. I suggested that he go into the GAP and then make a request to be shown any remaining energy of the fear of being vulnerable. I instructed him to notice the energy that came up in his body and then to shift to the CORE Technique when he became aware of where it was being held. I explained that as the energy dissolved he would either notice that it was gone, or that he might become absorbed in thinking thoughts about something else. He did this, and after a time reported that he had indeed become absorbed in thinking. When he became aware of this, he then went back into Pure Awareness using the GAP technique and again made the request to be shown any remaining energy related to the fear of vulnerability. After several iterations of this process, he again asked to be shown any remaining energy of the fear of being vulnerable, and this time nothing presented itself. It was just quiet and peaceful inside.

He then had the realization that he could now be fully present and self-expressed under any circumstances and felt completely free of any fear of vulnerability. The release of this deeply held but hidden fear was profound for him. When it was gone, he just laughed and laughed for several minutes because it was such a huge relief to be free of something that he hadn't even known he had been holding onto his whole life!

The Cycle of GAP, Provocation, CORE, Thoughts, Awareness

The key to success with the GPS Technique is to cycle through the sequence of its steps repeatedly until when you ask to be shown any remaining energy of the emotion, you get... nothing. Just to be sure I suggest that you make the request again. If you get nothing the second time, you are really complete with it!

This is an iterative process. You do the sequence of the GAP Technique, making your provocation request and then shifting to the CORE Technique as soon as you are shown where the energy is located in your body. Sometimes when you finish feeling into the energy using the CORE Technique and the energy is gone you are clearly in the state of Pure Awareness. If it happens like this, as soon as you are aware that the experience of the energy has been completed you'll notice that there is just the silence of Pure Awareness and you can make your request again.

Sometimes however when you are feeling into the energy with the CORE Technique you will notice after some time that you have drifted off into thinking about something else. You will reach a point where you realize that you are thinking. This is a natural process that I explained in the section about thoughts during the GAP Technique. These thoughts are the expression of the physical activity of the release of stresses in the body and they can create so much activity in the mind that you become absorbed in thinking for some time. It doesn't matter how long you were lost in thought, what matters is that when you become aware that you are thinking that you use the GAP Technique again. Begin once more to notice the background of silence in which these thoughts were occurring and when you have a clear experience of Pure Awareness again, make your request to become aware of any remaining energy related to the issue at hand. If there's anything left, the body will again show you where the energy is and you can shift to the CORE Technique.

So the process goes round and round from GAP, to your request to be aware of the energy, to the CORE, to either Pure Awareness or Thoughts and then Pure Awareness, and again back to the start with the GAP again.

GPS and the SEE Technique

You can also use the GPS Technique in combination with the SEE Technique instead of with the CORE Technique. When you go into Pure Awareness using the GAP as you would normally, then you make your request to see the energy of any remaining reaction to a particular unmet expectation or to the projection of a possible negative outcome onto the future. You can also use it for accessing subtle emotional energies associated with identifications that don't seem like they have any emotional charge to them.

When you get access to the pattern of energy, then shift to the SEE Technique and take your awareness out beyond the outer edge of the field of energy that is radiating out from the body into the environment. When you take your awareness out past the outer edge of the energy of the reaction you will be in Pure Awareness and the energy will simply fade away.

When the energy is gone you will be in Pure Awareness again and you can again make your request. Do this until you make your request twice and get no response. Then you are finished with this issue. There are no more "dust bunnies" of identification, attachment, projection, expectation or reaction to the issue. You will then notice that the story that was creating these illusions now looks pretty ridiculous. You won't waste your energy creating those fields of energy that radiate out from your body like that any more. You are free.

Remembering to use the GPS Technique

A good way to remember to use the GPS Technique is to make a habit of using it after the CORE and SEE Techniques as a way to make sure that you really resolved all of the energy related to the issue that you were working on. Sometimes you will feel into the

CORE of something and it will seem resolved. But doing the GPS will help you make sure that there are no existing backup copies of the energy, or closely related patterns of energy, still lurking inside of you somewhere. It's good to be free of all of the residual energy if there is any there. The GPS is a great vacuum cleaner technique!

How the GPS Technique Impacts Your Life

GPS is a great way to make sure you have really felt every aspect of any previously incomplete emotional experience. It is also a great way to get access to incompletions that you can't name or describe with words. It is a subtle and powerful Pure Awareness Technique.

As you use it you will find that your internal emotional landscape will become cleaner and cleaner. You'll feel this as a kind of lightness of your inner state of being. You will also feel a greater confidence when you complete something using the CORE or SEE Techniques as you follow it up with GPS. You'll know you really got it all.

Leaving residual patterns of energy in your body, be they incompletions or reactions just perpetuates them. They are your barriers to experiencing and enjoying the full presence of Pure Awareness all the time. So the GPS is your insurance policy for helping you to really get to the state in which you live from Pure Awareness all the time, as quickly as possible.

Integrating the Pure Awareness Techniques into Your Life

You can't learn to play the piano or guitar without practicing. In order to integrate Pure Awareness into your life and to realize the beautiful benefits of having a life grounded in that state of being, is to finally be able to actualize the promises made by all of the spiritual and personal development programs that you have studied in the past.

The Pure Awareness Techniques are what has been missing, and now you have them. Now the only thing you have to do is to use them every time there is an opportunity to do so.

What we are seeing now is that people who practice the Pure Awareness Techniques whenever they are needed are beginning to experience living from Pure Awareness most of the time. And it is happening much more quickly than from any other practice or program that I have heard of. Many people are showing genuine signs of stabilizing their experience of Pure Awareness within months of beginning to practice these techniques regularly.

It's not difficult to do this because the techniques themselves are not difficult. They are simple. Anyone who is interested in improving their life, in having breakthroughs that they just couldn't get before, now have an incredible set of techniques that when applied can transform their lives. Anyone interested in having a new depth of inner peace and happiness can have this by simply doing these techniques whenever one of life's hiccups comes along.

All you really have to do is to decide that you are going to do this. Simply decide to do the Pure Awareness Techniques whenever they are appropriate or needed. Make the decision and then do them. That's all you have to do to liberate yourself from the grip of emotion, from the grip of your conditioning and illusions. Freedom from suffering is well within your grasp. It doesn't really take much to step out of your old ways of being into a whole new way of life based on the reality of your own essential nature.

Getting More Support

In the beginning of learning and practicing these techniques it is a good idea to stack the cards in your favor for success. To do this it is ideal to hire a Core Dynamics Coach if you can afford to do so. Core Dynamics Coaches are well trained and certified in coaching using the Pure Awareness Techniques. You can find out more about hiring a Core Dynamics Coach at: www.thepowerofhow.com.

Another thing you can do is start a "Power of How" study group. Find some like-minded people who want to integrate the Pure Awareness Techniques into their life and get really good at using and benefiting from them. Get together either in person, on the phone or on line, and share your experiences and support each other. Help each other practice the Pure Awareness Techniques so everyone in the study group gets really good at them. It's a great way to keep you in the conversation and help you to remember to use the Pure Awareness Techniques. You can start or find a Power of How study group at www.thepowerofhow.com.

There is also more information about specific applications of Human Software Engineering at the Great Life Technologies web site at www.greatlifetechnologies.com. In addition, there is a special web site for my book, Vaporize Your Anxiety without Drugs or Therapy www.VaporizeYourAnxiety.com. We are scheduled to conduct a scientific study that will measure to what extent the Pure Awareness Techniques can reduce anxiety with a leading university researcher on anxiety disorders. The study is expected to be completed in the Fall of 2009. If you'd like the get the news about that and other developments at Great Life Technologies make sure to join our mailing list on any of the web pages at www.greatlifetechnologies.com.

Using the Pure Awareness Techniques during Core Dynamics Coaching

If you do hire a Core Dynamics Coach to help you learn and apply the Pure Awareness Techniques in your life, doing so will maximize your rate of progress in being able to live from Pure Awareness all the time. Plus, you will get superb guidance and support. Not only will you learn the techniques but your Core Dynamics Coach will also help you to identify your patterns of conditioning that are in the way of having the life you want. Core Dynamics Coaches are trained in a special protocol that rapidly pinpoints and accesses any unresolved emotional pain. They can help you find any remaining identifications, expectations and projections that are keeping you stuck in the illusion of being your ego. Having a Core Dynamics Coach assist you with the process of removing the basis of your inner conflicts, barriers and illusions is probably the fastest way to cultivate a new state of being in which you live from Pure Awareness all the time.

It is also a good idea to hire a Certified Core Dynamics Coach if you get stuck or have any trouble learning or using the Pure Awareness Techniques. Sometimes there are subtleties to what is keeping you stuck that you may not be able to see yourself, and having a Core Dynamics Coach help you will be the quickest and best solution.

What is Life Like when You Live from Pure Awareness all the Time?

It is clear what the barriers and reasons are that keep people from living from Pure Awareness all the time, and why this state of affairs is so common in the world. And now it's possible with the development of the new technologies of Human Software Engineering for anyone with the desire to quickly begin to dismantle these barriers and live more and more from Pure Awareness. By using these techniques, the day will come when even the illusory sense that you are an isolated individual will dissolve, and you will awaken to the reality that you are Pure Awareness and that Pure Awareness is all there really is.

What is it like to live in such a state?

- You always trust and act on your intuition

- You are always true to yourself

- You feel a deep capacity for intimacy and at the same time feel totally independent and self-sufficient

- You enjoy being completely free from the influences of the past and you have no worries or concerns about the future

- You experience total presence and live fully aware and present in every moment

- You never get lost to the grip of emotion

- You experience emotions fully, much more fully and richly than ever before but you don't get lost to them

- You have a natural capacity to feel anything and everything, making sensory experiences more alive and rich than you ever imagined was possible

- You feel a deep sense of oneness with nature and the universe

- You feel a natural alignment with and full support of all the laws of nature

- Your life feels like it is a continuous experience of being "in the Zone"

- You spontaneously function in alignment with nature and it feels as if you are an agent of nature and the universe

- You have a profound, unshakable inner sense of peace and harmony with everything

- Life is frictionless and things happen as if by magic in ways that you could never have imagined, and yet it all feels natural and perfect

- You feel a pervasive sense of permanent inner peace

- You feel completely free

- Your desires get fulfilled effortlessly and you are unattached to how and when they get fulfilled

- You have no problem with waiting when that is needed, and it doesn't feel like waiting because you are unattached to expectations; in fact you have given up the habit of creating and being attached to expectations altogether

- You feel a sense of oneness with unlimited power

- You feel unconditional love for everyone, even though you still have likes and preferences

- The experience of perpetual bliss is always present

And interestingly, as your entire inner landscape is dominated by Pure Awareness, on the outside you look just like a regular old human being, just like your neighbor. Granted, when people interact with you they feel that there is something very special about you. You seem to have very clean energy. You don't seem to be bothered by anything. You have something that they want but they can't put their finger on what it is.

This is what it's like. How do I know this? Well, you remember from earlier in the book when I said that experience is the basis of true knowing and full understanding? I wouldn't have this clarity if it wasn't coming from direct experience.

But don't take my word for it. Experience it yourself. All you have to do is start using the Pure Awareness Techniques. If you want to really put booster rockets on and accelerate things even more, work with a Core Dynamics Coach or a WaveMaker Coach and go through a systematic process of debugging and upgrading your inner human software. Have the intention of removing every conceivable barrier to living from Pure Awareness all the time. This can get you there even faster than just waiting for circumstances to bring up your unresolved stuff to remind you to use the techniques.

Now you know what is possible. Now you have the tools and techniques to remove the barriers to living from Pure Awareness all the time. It's there in the background, just on the other side of your incompletions. Why not dismantle them quickly, easily and completely so that you too can enjoy the continuous experience of Wholeness and Fulfillment for the rest of your life?

I hope that you will practice the Pure Awareness Techniques, and I hope that you will take advantage of the other incredible resources available to you from Great Life Technologies. Please visit our web site at www.greatlifetechnologies.com. Join our email list (which you can do at the site) so that you get our newsletters and announcements. Enjoy the other applications of Human Software Engineering and stay tuned as more amazing applications are developed.

Also, please check out the links in the Internet Resources section that follows. These links will guide you to detailed information about some other life changing applications that are not covered in this book.

My wish for you is that you live and enjoy the totality of who and what you really are. May you always enjoy experiencing and living from your essential nature...

Pure Awareness

What We Really Want

It's very simple. What we want as human beings is to feel good. That's ultimately what all of us really want. That means that we want to have wonderful experiences and enjoy our life as much as possible. We don't want suffering or pain or to be the victim of our circumstances. Instead we want to live life free from suffering.

Life does bring us a multitude of experiences. Some of them we like and others we don't. Regardless of what kind of experiences life brings us, there is one thing that we can do to avoid suffering and be in a state of fulfillment. That one thing is to always make the distinction between the circumstances that we find ourselves in and our reaction to those circumstances. We may or may not be able to do anything about the circumstances, but now that you have the powerful tools of the Pure Awareness Techniques you can certainly do something about your reaction to them.

Pain and suffering are not the same thing. Pain is simply a sensation. Suffering is our reaction to the pain. In order to maximize our experience of living a happy and fulfilling life, we can reduce or eliminate the element of suffering by simply using the Pure Awareness Techniques. Often this will resolve the pain itself, but even if it doesn't, it is still possible not to suffer even while there is pain in your body.

You will have challenges and circumstances occur in your life that you don't seem to have any control over. That's part of being human. But you don't have to suffer any more no matter what happens. Suffering comes from the loss of wholeness. Now that you know how to directly experience wholeness, you don't have to suffer any more.

My wish for you is that you truly master all eight of the Pure Awareness Techniques so that you can have a life free of suffering, free of the insidious limitations of the Core Dynamics, a life in which you are completely free to express the fullness of your being, the fullness of the unique expression of Pure Awareness that you are.

Oh, and don't forget to share these wonderful techniques with everyone you know. They are far too precious to keep them to yourself.

chapter 6

Pure Awareness
Techniques Stories

There are now thousands of people practicing the Pure Awareness
Techniques and liberating themselves from their suffering and
illusions. The following are just a few of the innumerable stories
of people using the Pure Awareness Techniques to come out of
the grip of their identifications and emotional pain into the light
of Pure Awareness. We are compiling more and more stories of
successes in personal awakening from using the Pure Awareness
Techniques. As you use the Pure Awareness Techniques and
experience your own liberation and awakening, if you'd like to
share your story for others to see on the Internet, please send it to;
info@greatlifetechnologies.com.

Pure Awareness Present Everywhere All the Time

Through using the Pure Awareness Techniques I have been able to finally attain
something I have wanted for so many years, which is to enjoy the experience of
Pure Awareness being present everywhere all the time.

So many people talk about it and I have met some mentors who actually
live it...but Tom Stone is the ONLY one who has developed such a precise,
powerful and assured way of identifying and removing the inner barriers of
incomplete experiences and identifications, that keep most of the world living
in turmoil and unnecessary stress and pain.

I now experience the world in a beautiful new way, free of inner conflicts - conflicts that use to cause me so much pain. Until now, I was never able to really resolve my inner conflicts and now I am free of them. I feel deeply in love with my life. The number one gift I gave to myself was to learn how to clear my energy and live in pure awareness. Until I did that my life was full of distractions and distortion.

Tom's ability to see and articulate the real nature of what was blocking me from experiencing Pure Awareness all the time is unique in the world today. He is such a master at this. I don't think there's a better guide.

Give yourself the gift of this life changing experience. Learn and practice the Pure Awareness Techniques. You will not regret it. The time is now. This is one area not to use the WAIT Technique on! Go for it."

– Michelle Humphrey

A Journey to Wholeness

There was always a sense that something was missing. A hole, an incompletion. A subtle need to look over the next hill to see if what was missing was there. It least, that's how it seemed to me. I could usually ignore the disquiet, but not always.

To compensate, I've always been a good thinker – bright enough, quick enough, well-read, logical and linear with a good ability to reason.

Not much for feelings though. I didn't even know how little I could feel. Subsequently I learned the reason I couldn't feel was because I couldn't afford to feel, for fear of being emotionally overwhelmed. But of course I didn't think there was any absence of feeling!

I used thinking to simulate feeling however, I found this to be slow, inaccurate, and ultimately misleading. It was, to paraphrase Shakespeare, sound and fury, signifying nothing.

I used thinking to pursue knowledge. Much study and training in, life planning, goal setting, NLP, several meditation techniques, clinical hypnosis, Time-Line Therapy and Silva. Each made some contribution to expanding my awareness. But there was still a "missing."

There were ten years spent studying, training, and being coached by Thomas Leonard, the founder of CoachU, CoachVille and the International Coach Federation that helped me develop a strong personal foundation, a clear platform from which to process my life and interact with the world. I experienced terrific growth and will always be grateful to him.

Then along came Tom Stone. Apparently I was ready for him because the journey to Wholeness accelerated. With Tom's guidance I've:

- Developed the direct experience of myself as a Being beyond the physical.

- Identified and resolved numerous pieces of stored conditioning which were blockages to living a satisfying, connected life. (An example is in the sidebar.)

- Diminished, virtually to the point of elimination, a sense of feeling separate from others and life. I now experience myself as "of" everything, everywhere, nearly all the time.

- Become a part of a process that gets easier the "higher" I go and which lifts me "higher" the easier it gets. Think about that. In "real" life we have to work harder to get further up the success ladder – more money, more freedom, and more power takes work. The inner process is exactly....not that! Each bit of awareness and growth lift me to a higher place where it's easier to become even more aware. It's as if I've climbed onto an upward-spiraling escalator.

- I react less, get upset less, respond quicker, take definitive actions sooner, and I am fundamentally more peaceful regardless of circumstances and events. It's as if I now see through the "noise" and more readily experience a wisdom, which permeates everything. My judgments about things – good/bad, right/wrong, moral/immoral – and my engagement with any "-ism's," have diminished.

- Reconciled the distinction between perfect and preferred, to wit, everything is perfect just the way it is; there's no reason for me to make anything wrong, nothing for me to push back against. At the same time I'm free to take action to change anything from the way it is now to a way I prefer it to be. This distinction is liberating and energizing for me.

This has led me, so far, to three cognitions.

First, I am whole and complete, innocent and pure, of All That Is, nothing missing, nothing broken, nothing needing to be healed. That is my essential nature, now and forever. I am completely nonphysical. This is not something I think is so; this is what I have awakened into experiencing. As you might imagine, this has been a pretty wonderful awakening.

Second, I am, at the same time, part of the physical dimensions of space and time. I bleed, laugh, feel, think, give, receive, screw up, contribute, suffer, and love. I stumble and soar. In short, I live the contrasts that are part of the manifesting universe. And I've learned to enjoy the contrasts, not just look for the "good" stuff.

Third, these two "versions" of me, the nonphysical and the physical, are equally important, contributing in different ways to my journey. Each – the inner and the outer – is connected to the other and are intertwined like the dual-helix strands of the DNA molecule. One strand, the inner me, represents my growth in the non-physical realm. The other strand represents my growth in the physical, here-and-there, now-and-then realm. The intertwined strands, together, represent Wholeness.

Perhaps the best thing about my journey to Wholeness is awakening to the awareness that everyone is already whole and complete. It awaits only our desire, intention, and action to experience it. Wholeness Is.

Close, dark, warm spaces emotional overwhelm.

For years I traveled extensively and frequently by commercial airplane. I loved the experience of flying and had no warning of the change that awaited me. One normal day I was scheduled to be on a flight from Denver back to Dallas. I was early to the boarding gate and had the opportunity to catch the last seat available on an earlier flight. Grabbing my carryon luggage I gratefully boarded, to be seated in the middle seat on the last row. Trading that mild inconvenience with the two-hours-earlier-home benefit was easy for me.

As I settled into to the seat I had a sudden powerful claustrophobic emotional reaction. I immediately stood up in the isle (climbing back over the poor guy I had just climbed over to be seated!) and started to try to calm my breathing. I was unsuccessful. Grabbing my bag I charged off the plane just before the door was closed.

Standing in the boarding gate area I calmed down, reconfirmed my seat on my original flight, and sat down to try to figure what the hell had just happened. The facts were – the plane was full, the air on the plane was warm and still, and the interior lights were not on so it was a dim space. Let's see, close, warm, dim. Who cares? Well I sure did! And I didn't understand why. To shorten the story, I went on home on a plane that was lightly loaded (no one in my row), bright, and cool. No problem.

Over subsequent months I had very few flights scheduled, thus had little opportunity to test my reactions. In the interim I tried several tools from my many trainings – visualization, focusing on positive outcomes, fear resolution, self-hypnosis, and other techniques. It's interesting to note that all of the techniques were thinking-based, mind processes. I found some relief but still dreaded boarding a plane even when going to some wonderful destination for fun.

After Tom and I started working together I shared this issue with him. We quickly eliminated many things. For instance, it really wasn't about claustrophobia. The elements of it seemed to be rooted so deeply in my mind/past/conditioning that it was literally un-understandable. Uh oh, I wasn't going to be able to figure this out, no thinking my way out of it. Other approaches were called for.

I began to master the Pure Awareness Techniques. Having the direct experience of my essential nature as existing beyond time and space established a liberating frame of reference from which to work. (One time I had what seemed like a "past life experience" of having been in the small cockpit of a World War II fighter which was on fire, dim due to the smoke, and crashed, killing me. Interesting. I make no claims about cause-and-effect for my current condition.)

I then begin to practice the CORE Technique whenever I could evoke the emotional reaction to thoughts of close, dark, warm spaces. Sometimes it was hard to conjure up the emotional feelings and other times it was easier. I later realized I was holding back because I feared being completely overwhelmed by them and feared I would literally lose my mind and enter a state from which I would be unable to return.

Bit by bit, however, I could feel changes occurring. I had more freedom and less fear of being in an overwhelming situation.

But finally I got tired of being held hostage....by me! One day, alone, sitting on the deck overlooking the lake I realized that it was now or never, victor or victim, free or bound, I had to go into the center of this and resolve it once and for all. It was the scariest thing I had ever done. Period. But I also knew by then, from practice, that the center of the most intense part of the energy that powered the emotion was the safest place to be, that as long as I could remain there I would not be grabbed by the emotion. Even knowing that, it was still a scary thing to do.

I made it. After an indeterminate length of time I broke out into Pure Awareness. Free! What a moving experience that was! No longer a victim of my conditioning, now free to be a creator. Wow!

To close this story, there are two things to share. First, I looked for opportunities to test my new state. My mantra was, Bring it on! I finally stopped this because it got boring. I'm done, no need to test it further.

The second thing is the effect this resolution has had on the rest of my life. I now do things I would have put off before. Need to have an unpleasant conversation? Just do it. Major business decision necessary? Handle it and move on. There seems to be nothing to fear anymore, only opportunities to create the life I'm really here to live.

I encourage you to learn the techniques in this book. Practice them. Master them. Live free.

– Steve Straus

I have stayed on a dietary program and lost 35 pounds

I was to nervous to disclose any underlying issues that may have been the hidden and root cause of my weight gain. Tom led me into a quiet meditation. Then he asked if I could recall a time when I felt the anxiety about eating.

The first thing I could vividly recall was that I could not go on any airline flight without having had a big meal or without also bringing aboard lots of snacks. I guess I had not been able to stand having no access to a refrigerator.

As I discussed my fear for the first time, Tom noticed a change in my tone of voice and asked if I could feel the energy of my anxiety and fear over not having access to food. I could.

With only that short preparation, Tom led me through the CORE Technique, allowing me to complete that feeling. The process totally eliminated that fearful issue. This was the beginning of the end of my self-medication with food.

For the first time, I was able to participate in a fasting regimen for an entire day. And I can now fly without bulking up prior to take off! And most significantly, I have stayed on a dietary program and lost 35 pounds.

– Cecelia Inwentarz

Doing this Work Automatically Teaches You to Love Yourself

Prior to reading the book, Pure Awareness, by Tom Stone, I already considered myself to be a completely happy and content person. I was fortunate enough to be exposed at a very young age to teachings of a spiritual nature. Gaining spiritual awareness has been a process for me that has occurred very slowly and has required an unwavering level of trust and commitment. Since graduating college I have been living with a lot of debt and have been relatively disillusioned with career life. I don't believe in having money problems or any type of problems. Problems are disguises for learning opportunities. The biggest hurdle I had to overcome was learning and trusting that my supply is not from my career, but is a result of being true to myself or living from a 'higher' standpoint.

I did have some challenges with my job however, as the company I worked for wasn't very employee friendly. I was being overburdened with work and feeling very helpless and frustrated all the time. In the spring of 2008 I learned of Tom Stone and Great Life Technologies. I decided to read Tom's book, Pure Awareness. I found the GAP Technique familiar and at the same time refreshing. It was reassuring that Tom believes it is so important to live in your Greater Awareness Place. I have lived my whole life in this 'Awareness' but never really conceptualized it the way it is described in Pure Awareness.

The technique that was completely new and foreign to me was the CORE Technique. Before I read Pure Awareness I always just embraced my feelings and acknowledged that they are there for me to learn from. I assumed they would eventually fade away. I would mildly resist the feelings but usually if I smiled in my head at them and asked myself why I was feeling a certain way I would get the answer within a short amount of time, sometimes right away or sometimes a few weeks or even months later. This method brought me to a point where most of my internal blockage has been cleared out slowly and arduously over the course of my life.

Once I learned about the CORE Technique I immediately started practicing it on a daily basis on my work frustrations. All the while I was trying to figure out how I could leave my relatively good paying job at the same time no companies were hiring. I didn't really know what I wanted to do. All of a sudden I woke up one morning and it occurred to me to travel overseas with my friends who were going to teach English in Korea. I love traveling and there is high demand for English teachers abroad. I looked into it and by August I put in my resignation at work and felt free. However, deep down I knew that going abroad was not the path for me. So I used the WAIT Technique and trusted that the right opportunity has already happened for me.

I ended up starting my own business and am now busy working for myself. I am now working less than I was at my old job and have more than doubled my income and I am freeing myself from my debt. Without Tom's book I know none of these great things would have happened so fast. The exciting part about this is that I don't even feel like I did anything or made any real effort towards creating the wonderful self-employment situation I am in.

Now when I am feeling any sort of negative feelings I use the CORE Technique and can usually wipe away negative emotions very quickly. I know they won't be bottled up and throwing me off balance in the future.

When living and implementing the Pure Awareness Techniques I know I am living true to myself. In my Greater Awareness Place I have gone from making decisions I think someone else wants me to make to making decisions that are right for me. The Pure Awareness Techniques have given me a profound sense of confidence and trust in myself.

In my opinion, the Pure Awareness Techniques are the most efficient techniques for helping people achieve the life they want by focusing within to manifest a perfect life, whatever that may be to each individual.

– Mike Redfield

Overcoming Thirty Years of Depression

When I was 2 years old my father died and as a result I suffered terrible feelings of insecurity, depression, anxiety, inferiority, low self-esteem and minimal confidence. I felt isolated and different from other children as I did not have a father. My school years were not good. I left school with few qualifications and ended up in a job that I thoroughly disliked with few prospects.

I was fortunate to be physically very fit and I exercised daily in order to alleviate my feelings of depression and anxiety. I left the job to follow my passion of teaching people the benefits of exercise through personal fitness training.

The depression I felt first occurred when I was fourteen, and continued for thirty years. Around this time, a magazine advertisement inspired me to attend a course aiming to help people remove the barriers in their life, for example, loosing weight by learning the Core Dynamics of Common Problems.

Becoming aware of these pure awareness techniques and learning to live in the present rather than the past and future has had an amazing effect on my life. I have so much more energy than I had previously and my self esteem and confidence has grown dramatically. My mind feels at ease and still, rather than the previous feeling of constantly dwelling on the past or worrying about the future.

I feel that the depression and anxiety I felt has been cured and I am now grateful for everything I have in life. I do not worry about anything anymore and I do not judge people like I used to. I do not dwell on any previous bad experiences. The Pure Awareness Techniques have been so much more effective than taking drugs to solve the negative emotions.

In addition to my fitness training business I have founded my own life and well being coaching business. My aim is to help others solve different issues that may occur in their lives.

Many thanks to Linda Mosely and Tom Stone for enlightenment.

– John Lingley

(Linda Mosely is a certified Core Dynamics Teacher and Coach in Oxford, England)

The Experience of Losing My Daughter and then Again...Not!

Several months ago I met Tom Stone through another successful coach who suggested that if I wanted to improve my coaching work I should take some of Tom's classes. Well I did and the results have been phenomenal.

I have used the CORE & SEE Techniques numerous times with my clients and they always experience release from heartbreak, pain and fear. My clients are amazed at how much better they feel and thank me repeatedly. I knew from these results I was doing the right thing.

But it's always different when challenges hit your home. About a year and a half ago I ended a seven-year relationship in which I was the surrogate father to her little girl.

I met my daughter when she was born. I call her my daughter even though I am her surrogate daddy. But to the two of us, she is my baby and I her daddy.

Our relationship as daddy and daughter grew tighter over the years and out lasted my relationship with her mother. But that was never a challenge for any of us as love and harmony were always the basis of our friendship and extended family.

Living several blocks away, afforded us the opportunity to always be together with sleepovers, soccer practice, dinners, home schooling and all the joys of life. For all practical reasons, I was to her the number one daddy in her life.

And then it happened. On a Saturday, just after soccer practice her mother called me and informed me that due to her new relationship, it was better for all that I not participate in my daughter's life. It was time to end my relationship with my daughter and allow mom and her new boyfriend to build their family. I would never be involved with her again.

I tried every thing to persuade her mom to at least let me say good-bye so that she would know that I had not abandoned her, but nothing worked. It was here that I had to face my pain.

First there was anger, tears and much sadness. And then, I decided to face it all in the only way I knew. I used Tom's feeling into the CORE & SEE Techniques to release the energetic pattern associated with the emotion in my body. It took several times, because I would bounce between the "story" and the heartache. But each time I would go into the CORE and the SEE Techniques to complete my experience. I was amazed how easily I let go of all the pain.

I can tell you that the anger, hurt and pain disappeared. So is the heartache. In its place is peace. I now understand the challenges that caused her mom to do what she did, and I am at peace with her too. She acted out of the highest level of love that she thought was appropriate at the time. I could not fault her; we all do this at one time or another in our lives. There is no blame.

I still love my daughter. That will never end. But now, there is a peace that can hold those years with my child in loving memories of her crawling onto my lap and the two of us sharing our love for one another. This relationship will last forever in my heart. It has no ending.

I also know that my daughter is released from her loss too. She knows I love her. And, she knows how to be Present. After all, I taught her that through Tom's work. I am so grateful.

Postscript: When we come to that place of Pure Awareness life as we know it changes. The Universe aligns events to reflect who we truly are. It shifts our experiences in ways we least expect.

Several months later, just after Christmas, there was a knock at my door. Standing there was my daughter and her Mom. After many hugs, kisses and unending chatter between my daughter and me, I looked up to see Mom whisper…"I'm sorry." All was forgiven. All was restored.

When we choose to be Present, "that which was in part, becomes whole". My daughter asked…"Daddy, did you have a good Christmas?" I replied from my heart….'every day is Christmas, sweetie."

– Robin Hill

No More Fainting When Getting My Blood Taken

For as long as I can remember I have fainted when getting my blood taken or when there was the prospect of getting my blood taken or having to be in a doctor's office. I have used what seems to be every technique possible to over come this reaction, including Past life regression analysis, Time Line therapy, EFT, etc.

Just recently I went in for my regular blood work analysis and once again began to feel light headed. This time it occurred to me that I should try the CORE Technique and feel into where this anxiety was coming from. I felt into a spot in my chest and I felt like a "pop" occurred. I could not find the anxiety and I was no longer light headed. I have since been in the doctor's office and visiting someone in the hospital and I was amazed that I no longer had any anxiety come up as I would have in the past.

– Rich Riedman

Able to Remain Present to Bliss and Joy in Spite of Difficult Times

I started practicing the Pure Awareness Techniques about a year ago. Prior to this I tried counseling, prescriptions, books, personal growth seminars, spiritual retreats and relied heavily on mentors.

Most of us have financial setbacks from time to time and the way I used to react to such a calamity was with anger, rage, and sometimes punching something within reach, such as a steering wheel or pillow. I would spend much of the day crying hysterically. My stomach felt horrible. I thought, there must be a way to avoid reacting this way, and in spite of all the work I was doing on myself, something was missing.

Since learning the Pure Awareness Techniques, I have noticed that when problematic situations come up I do not have the same feelings of despair and hysteria. There have been many serious challenges in the last three months and they just don't feel like challenges. Life feels great. My daughter and I were to have a house of our own and the deal fell through. When I got that phone call, it felt just like any other day. I didn't cry. I did not even feel like crying. I even remained cheerful.

Since then we've been staying with friends. I began saving money to rent a home and got very close to my target amount. Just yesterday, I found out that my bank accounts were frozen by a credit card company I owed money to from a business I owned almost seven years ago. I went through a divorce, lost my business and I was unable to re-pay the debt. All the money I saved up, plus money I need to pay current bills, was gone.

Even as I write this, outstanding checks are hitting the accounts and fees are mounting. According to my lawyers, the creditor will get every dime of the money in my account and I will never see it again. In the past this would have been devastating. While it is definitely unpleasant, I have not become angry, I have not punched anything, I have not cried hysterically. I did shed a couple of tears and before they even dried up, I began to see the beauty in much of the process, ways that the blow was softened, and blessings that are still keeping us very much afloat in spite of the freeze.

My intuition (which is much easier to hear clearly after using the Pure Awareness Techniques) led me through a series of actions which resulted in me finding out much sooner than I would have if I had followed my normal daily routine. This gave me time to cancel direct deposits, sit down with my banker, talk to lawyers, make necessary phone calls and spend a nice evening with my daughter. Because of the Pure Awareness Techniques I was able to remain present to bliss and joy in spite of what was happening around me. Today I am penniless and homeless, and yet these have been the best three months of my life. My friendships with those who opened their homes to us have strengthened and grown in many beautiful ways. I am so excited to see what happens in the future when this temporary situation shifts to the manifestation of all the wonderful things to come.

– Melaney Gabris

I Fully Live in the Power of Now - I Am Free

Human Software Engineering has allowed me to fully live in the power of now. Life flows with ease and everyday is so exciting. There is no more need to feel like a victim, to be right, to be anything. The voice of my ego is like that of the child I once was in a distant memory. I hear it speak and I reply from my knowing. This communication resonates with the same set rhythm and tone as the conversations I have with my granddaughter.

Patiently, I observe the three year old speaking in me. I understand the pain and the fear and I know it is all energy. The energy of the experiences, interpretations and beliefs of the three year old is there in me. I am the observer who knows this is just an illusion and I know exactly how to exchange this energy for a higher vibration, using the Pure Awareness Techniques. It is as simple as feeling right down into the core of the energy of the feeling and voila; I come to a different place. I am no longer tangled in my ego. I am free.

– Donna Anderson

chapter 7

Internet Resources

The main web site for accessing additional resources related to the Power of How is located at www.thepowerofhow.com. To gain access to all of the resources and the Power of How social network you will need to register. We will not rent or sell your email address to anyone and you can unsubscribe from the list at anytime.

Once registered you will have access to recordings of examples of people being guided through the Pure Awareness Techniques. In the social networking section you can find and connect with other readers of the Power of How, join or form a Power of How study group, invite your friends and make new friends who are interested in gaining mastery of the Pure Awareness Techniques and living from Pure Awareness all the time. You can check out and sign up for Core Dynamics Coaching. By registering you'll be on the Power of How mailing list so that we can let you know about Power of How seminars and other events and news related to the Power of How.

The Great Life Technologies web site is located at: www.greatlifetechnologies.com. You can join our email list to receive our free newsletters about new developments in Human Software Engineering and Great Life Technologies events and programs. The web site and newsletters are rich resources of information about the many applications of Human Software Engineering.

The Great Life Coaching Web Site - www.greatlifecoaching.com

This is the place to get connected with coaches who have been trained and certified by Great Life Technologies to provide Core Dynamic Coaching and WaveMaker Coaching.

The coaching programs include:

Core Dynamics Coaching

WaveMaker Coaching

The Be Smoke Free Now Program
(a powerful WaveMaker and Pure Awareness Techniques based smoking cessation program that is amazingly effective for helping people easily and quickly become non-smokers for the rest of their life)

Extraordinary Wellness Coaching:
(Core Dynamics and WaveMaker based coaching for resolving the underlying inner conflicts that keep people from getting well)

Extraordinary Relationship Coaching:
(resolve your resentments, improve your communication, learn to be both intimate and independent, find the ideal partner if you're single, etc.)

Extraordinary Prosperity Coaching:
(our conditioning around money issues is thick and deep. Work with a Core Dynamics or WaveMaker Coach to remove all of the conditioning that gets in the way of truly prospering on all levels of your life)

And more...

Articles by Tom Stone:

http://greatlifetechnologies.com/articlesindex.shtml

This link is to an index of articles written by Tom Stone on various aspects of Human Software Engineering and other related topics.

Join the free Human Software Engineering Yahoo email discussion group:

http://health.groups.yahoo.com/group HumanSoftwareEngineering

Join the hundreds of people who are discussing Human Software Engineering in all of its many applications. Search the many years of archives with keywords for topics of interest.

The Peace of Mind Program:

http://greatlifetechnologies.com/PeaceOfMindQuickUpgrade.shtml

Have one of the primary underlying causes of ADD and ADHD debugged via HSE Resonance Drops that can be individualized for you and sent to you via the mail.

The Squeaky Clean Program:

http://greatlifetechnologies.com/SqueakyCleanProgram.shtml

Learn about the brilliant insights of leading European researchers and practitioners who have been using HSE devices for decades to remove the underlying causes of chronic diseases, allergies, toxins, pathogens, etc. This is a program to get well and stay well. It is also available remotely via HSE Resonance Drops.

Core Dynamics Coach Training:

http://greatlifetechnologies.com/CDCTraining/Options.html

How would you like to make a great living helping people remove their inner barriers to having the life they truly want. Core Dynamics Coaching uses the Pure Awareness Techniques to resolve inner barriers faster and more completely than any other form of coaching or therapy. It's setting a new standard of coaching. This training prepares you for certification by the International Coaching Federation as well as by Great Life Technologies.

The WaveMaker Mastery Program:

http://greatlifetechnologies.com/NewMasteryProgram.html

A six month mentoring program taught by Tom Stone and members of the Mastery Team. This training not only teaches you to be a superb WaveMaker Coach but also helps you clean out your own inner barriers so that you show up as clean as possible to serve each of your coaching clients. You become someone who people want to be coached by. They get the feeling of – I'll have what she's having!

The 12 Core Dynamics of Common Problems - Audio CD set

http://greatlifetechnologies.com/CoreDynamicsCDSet.html

The 12 Core Dynamics of Common Problems two-day seminar given by Tom Stone - Learn all 12 Core Dynamics insights into the nature of human conditioning in depth and also hear additional examples of the first Five Pure Awareness Technique directly from Tom.

Appendix: The Essence of Each Core Dynamic

Overcoming the 12 Core Barriers to Living and Enjoying Pure Awareness

To be learned for each Barrier to living and enjoying Pure Awareness:

- **The Core Dynamic**
    - This is the way of being that has resulted from our pre-verbal conditioning

- **The Feeling Level Decision**
    - This is the decision that is made on a feeling level that has no words to it that becomes the basis of how we limit our experiences of life

- **The Conditioned Response**
    - This is the specific learned reactive behavior based on the Feeling Level Decision

- **Knowing the Distinction between**
    - This is what is important to intellectually understand in order to recognize the Conditioned Response, and be able to use the appropriate Pure Awareness Technique

- What needs to be learned?

    - This is the combination of becoming aware of our previously unconscious conditioned responses and consciously choosing in that moment of awareness to cultivate a new way of being

    - **What needs to be optimized?**

    - This is the description of the capacity or skill that needs to be cultivated and mastered in order to fully live the new way of being

- **The Pure Awareness Technique**

    - This is the specific Experiential Technique that is to be learned and used to dissolve the Conditioned Responses that create this Core Dynamic

The 12 Core Dynamics of Common Problems

1 – Resisting Feeling Things Fully
- The Conditioning of Avoiding Emotional Overwhelm

2 – Ignoring Your Intuition
- The Conditioning of Doubt

3 – Being Judgmental
- The Conditioning of Separateness

4 – Avoiding the Present
- The Conditioning of Distractions and Addictions

5 – Looking for Yourself Where You Are Not
- The Conditioning of Longing

6 – Mistaking Need for Love
- The Conditioning of Dependence

7 – Resisting Change
- The Conditioning of Control

8 – Limiting Self-expression
- The Conditioning of Holding Back

9 – Trying to Force the Outcome
- The Conditioning of Forcing

10 – Excluding Other Perspectives
- The Conditioning of Attachment and Ego

11 – Manufacturing Interpretations
- The Conditioning of Misinterpretation

12 – Over-reacting to Circumstances
- The Conditioning of Reactivity

Details of the 12 Core Dynamics
The Barriers to Living and Enjoying Pure
Awareness All the Time

Barrier 1
The Conditioning of Avoiding Emotional Overwhelm

- The Core Dynamic
  - Resisting Feeling Things Fully

- The Feeling Level Decision
  - To limit our access to our capacity to feel in an attempt to avoid getting emotionally overwhelmed

- The Conditioned Response
  - To avoid all possible situations where there might be a chance of getting emotionally overwhelmed

- Knowing the Distinction between
  - Feeling and Emotion

- What needs to be learned?
  - How to dissolve the unresolved emotional energies that we hold in our bodies from the past and allow ourselves to feel everything fully

- What needs to be optimized?
  - Access to Your Innate Ability to Know Through Direct Experience

- The Pure Awareness Technique
  - CORE – Center of Remaining Energy - Feeling into the Core of the Energy of the Feeling

- When this Dynamic is Absent
    - I feel anything and everything without the fear of being overwhelmed

Barrier 2
The Conditioning of Doubt

- The Core Dynamic
    - Ignoring Your Intuition

- The Feeling Level Decision
    - To avoid acting on our intuition/inner knowing in an attempt to avoid getting emotionally overwhelmed in response to punishment or confrontation

- The Conditioned Response
    - To have an intuitive knowing but not trust it, not act on it and later to regret this
    - To avoid confrontation
    - To not stand up for yourself, not be true to yourself

- Knowing the Distinction between
    - Knowing and Thinking
    - Intuition and Emotional Impulsiveness

- What needs to be learned?
    - How to remember the future as clearly as the past without negating it
    - How to dissolve the unresolved emotional energies that we hold in our bodies from the past related to the fear of being emotionally overwhelmed by punishment, anger, guilt, confrontation, manipulation, etc.

- How to be able to simply stay present when someone else is upset even if they are directing their upset at you

- To know that the other person's upset or threat of confrontation is their own conditioned response that is being used to try to control/manipulate you. It is their problem not yours that they don't like it when you are being true
to yourself

- **What needs to be optimized?**
  - Your ability to act on your intuition every single time

- **The Pure Awareness Technique**
  - CORE – Center of Remaining Energy - Feeling into the Core of the Energy of the Feeling

  - To be used to dissolve the fear of being overwhelmed by punishment or confrontation when you are true to yourself

- **When this Dynamic is Absent**
  - I completely trust my intuition and I always act on it

Barrier 3
The Conditioning of the Illusion of Separateness

- **The Core Dynamic**
  - Being Judgmental

- **The Feeling Level Decision**
  - I can't feel and resolve issues within myself so I'll simply judge others as wrong or bad for having the same or similar issues

- **The Conditioned Response**
    - To create an illusion that the issue that I need to acknowledge and resolve within myself is in someone else and not in me.
    - To avoid acknowledging and resolving such issues for fear of getting emotionally overwhelmed

- **Knowing the Distinction between**
    - Being Discerning and Being Judgmental

- **What needs to be learned?**
    - How to get the maximum value out of every experience in life
    - How to dissolve the unresolved emotional energies in us that are triggered by seeing a similar pattern in others
    - How to be able to see everything in life as a mirror of ourselves

- **What needs to be optimized?**
    - Your ability to see perfection in everything
    - Your ability to see the world as a mirror

- **The Pure Awareness Technique**
    - Feeling into the Core of the Energy of the Feeling
    - To be used to dissolve the unresolved issues within ourselves that trigger our judgmental behavior and attitudes and cause us to create the illusion that this issue is in the other and not in us

- **When this Dynamic is Absent**
    - Everything I experience is a part of me. I acknowledge it, embrace it and value from it

Barrier 4
The Conditioning of Distractions and Addictions

- **The Core Dynamic**
  - Avoiding the Present

- **The Feeling Level Decision**
  - To avoid having your awareness be fully in the present because of the fear of being emotionally overwhelmed by the feelings that are there to be felt in that moment

- **The Conditioned Response**
  - To minimize awareness of the feelings that are in the present (even if these are unresolved feeling from the past) by
  - distracting ourselves with absorption in stories about the past or future
  - numbing out via a drug of choice/addictive behavior

- **Knowing the Distinction between**
  - Presence and Pain

- **What needs to be learned?**
  - How to be fully present to every experience in the now
  - How to access and utilize your capacity to stay present and feel what is there to be felt in the moment

- **What needs to be optimized?**
  - Your ability to stay present even when the experiences are intense

- **The Pure Awareness Technique**
  - CORE – Center of Remaining Energy - Feeling into the Core

of the Energy of the Feeling

- To be used to complete the unresolved emotional energies from the past that we become aware of when we allow our awareness to be fully in the now

- **When this Dynamic is Absent**
  - I live completely in the present moment

Barrier 5
The Conditioning of Longing

- **The Core Dynamic**
  - Looking for Yourself Where You Are Not

- **The Feeling Level Decision**
  - Part of me that is associated with my needs getting met is missing and I won't be complete until I find/have that missing part of me. It's out here somewhere. If only I could find it, then I would be whole.

- **The Conditioned Response**
  - To try to get part of the sense of yourself from things outside of you

  - To long for something to make you feel complete and fulfilled

  - To look to others for

    - Validation

    - Approval

    - Respect

    - Love

    - Etc.

- **Knowing the Distinction between**
  - Pure Awareness and All Other Experiences

- **What needs to be learned?**
  - How to enjoy the inner peace of self-sufficiency
  - How to experience the true nature of yourself independent of anything outside of you
  - How to become grounded in the experience of your essential nature such that you never lose the awareness of it

- **What needs to be optimized?**
  - Self-reliance and independence

- **The Pure Awareness Techniques**
  - GAP – Greater Awareness Place - Experiencing Pure Awareness in the Gap Between Thoughts
    - To provide the direct experience of the essential nature of what you really are
    - This gives the direct experience of the Self as Wholeness
  - SEE – Side Entrance Expansion – Extracting Your Awareness from being collapsed inside the energy field of an identification, reaction or projection
    - To come out of the grip of an emotional reaction
    - To experience Pure Awareness juxtaposed with the energy of your emotional reaction
    - To release yourself from identification with the story at the basis of your reaction

- **When this Dynamic is Absent**
  - I am whole and complete

Barrier 6
The Conditioning of Dependence

- **The Core Dynamic**
  - Mistaking Need for Love

- **The Feeling Level Decision**
  - If my needs are not getting met, I am not loved.

- **The Conditioned Response**
  - To become identified with and/or attached to the object of our needs getting met under the illusion that what we are feeling is love

  - To chase after getting our emotional needs met in order to feel loved

  - To attempt to meet other peoples needs so that they will love us

- **Knowing the Distinction between**
  - Love and Need

- **What needs to be learned?**
  - How to continuously experience the state of unconditional love within yourself

  - How to have a life filled with love

- **What needs to be optimized?**
  - the state of being unconditional love

- **The Pure Awareness Techniques**
  - GAP – Greater Awareness Place - Experiencing Pure Awareness in the Gap Between Thoughts
    - To provide the direct experience that your essential nature is pure unconditional love
    - This gives the direct experience of the Self as Pure Love
  - SEE – Side Entrance Expansion – Extracting Your Awareness from being collapsed inside the energy field of an identification, reaction or projection
    - To resolve emotional neediness, attachment and identification
    - To experience Pure Awareness juxtaposed with the energy of need or dependence
    - To experientially release yourself from need and attachment and become grounded in the independence and self-sufficiency of your true inner nature
  - CORE – Center of Remaining Energy - Feeling into the Core of the Feeling of the fear of not being loved or the fear of not having your needs met
    - To resolve any unresolved emotional energies from the past that are barriers to living in a state of unconditional love

- **When this Dynamic is Absent**
  - I love without needing anything in return and I participate in relationships of mutual giving
  - I experience my inner reality as unconditional love

- The distinction between love and need is completely clear to me

Barrier 7
The Conditioning of Control

- **The Core Dynamic**
    - Resisting Change

- **The Feeling Level Decision**
    - I need to keep things the same in order to feel secure

- **The Conditioned Response**
    - To attempt to control things, events and people in order to have the illusion of safety
    - To feel that the sense of who I am is threatened by too much change
    - To become comfortable with old habits, even though they are awful or ineffective, simply because there is a familiarity and reliability of them being the same as before

- **Knowing the Distinction between**
    - The non-changing nature of pure awareness and the changing nature of all other experiences – even if they have been around for a long time and seem not to be changing

- **What needs to be learned?**
    - How to have a natural inner sense of security
    - How to recognize our attempts to control our experiences

- How to live in the wonder and delight of uncertainty

- **What needs to be optimized?**
    - Your capacity to thrive during change by being grounded in Pure Awareness

- **The Pure Awareness Techniques**
    - GAP – Greater Awareness Place - Experiencing Pure Awareness in the Gap Between Thoughts
        - To provide the direct experience that your essential nature is the only thing that doesn't change

    - SEE – Side Entrance Expansion – Extracting Your Awareness from being collapsed inside the energy field of an identification, reaction or projection
        - To resolve expectations of trying to keep things from changing
        - To resolve the tendency to project possible negative outcomes onto the future
        - To resolve the fear of not knowing who you are if you let go of long-standing identifications

    - AGAPE – Accessing Greater Awareness Place Everywhere - Experiencing Pure Awareness Everywhere
        - To provide the direct experience that your essential nature provides you with a stable basis and reference of non-change

    - CORE – Center of Remaining Energy - Feeling into the Core of the Feeling
        - To resolve the fear of change or the fear of loss of sense of self

- **When this Dynamic is Absent**
    - I have a deep inner sense of equanimity.
    - I live in the delight and wonder of uncertainty.

Barrier 8
The Conditioning of Holding Back

- **The Core Dynamic**
    - Limiting Self-expression

- **The Feeling Level Decision**
    - If I am powerfully self-expressed, I'll lose the connection to those whom I depend on for a sense of being loved, accepted, approved of, and who give me a sense of belonging
    - If I really express myself powerfully I will be abandoned

- **The Conditioned Response**
    - To play the game of "let's all stay mediocre together"
    - To avoid doing those things that would be powerful self-expression in order not to alienate friends and family
    - To not "put yourself out there" for fear of rejection or criticism

- **Knowing the Distinction between**
    - True independence and needing others to approve of you and accept you

- **What needs to be learned?**
  - That what you are getting from others is not love
  - How to be powerfully self-expressed regardless of how others respond to this
  - How to feel so secure within yourself that you don't need the illusion of getting love/connection/acceptance/ approval from others

- **What needs to be optimized?**
  - The courage to be creative and fully self-expressed
    - The ability to handle other people being disturbed by your self-expression and have it be truly their problem without it impacting you or holding you back

  - The Pure Awareness Techniques
    - GAP – Greater Awareness Place - Experiencing Pure Awareness in the Gap Between Thoughts
    - To provide the direct experience that your essential nature is where acceptance and approval become non-issues

  - AGAPE – Accessing Greater Awareness Place Everywhere - Experiencing Pure Awareness Everywhere
    - To provide the direct experience of the self-sufficient nature of Pure Awareness which is the foundation for full self expression

  - SEE – Side Entrance Expansion – Extracting Your Awareness from being collapsed inside the energy field of an identification, reaction or projection

- To resolve projections that others won't like it if you are powerfully self-expressed

- CORE – Center of Remaining Energy - Feeling into the Core of the Feeling

- To resolve the fear of being abandoned

- **When this Dynamic is Absent**
  - I can be fully self expressed without fearing the loss of love from others

Barrier 9
The Conditioning of Forcing

- **The Core Dynamic**
  - Trying to Force the Outcome

- **The Feeling Level Decision**
  - If I don't make it happen, it won't happen
  - I am the doer
  - I am my ego
  - I am separate from others and everything

- **The Conditioned Response**
  - To create expectations and try to control events to be the way you think they should be
  - To make decisions from thinking and emotion rather than from knowing
  - To be reactive

- To see life as a struggle for survival
- To feel victimized, rebellious and at odds with life

- **Knowing the Distinction between**
  - Persistence and Forcing

- **What needs to be learned?**
  - How to live and work in the zone
  - That you are Pure Awareness and not your ego, your intellect, your stories, your emotional reactions, your perspective, your expectations or your projections

- **What needs to be optimized?**
  - Your ability to wait for clarity
  - Your ability to always have perfect timing
  - Your alignment with the law of least effort

- **The Pure Awareness Techniques**
  - GAP – Greater Awareness Place - Experiencing Pure Awareness in the Gap Between Thoughts
    - To provide the direct experience of what you really are
  - AGAPE – Accessing Greater Awareness Place Everywhere - Experiencing Pure Awareness Everywhere
    - To provide the direct experience that you are the Universe
    - To provide the direct experience of your oneness with everything
    - To provide the direct experience of the place that Knowing comes from

- SEE – Side Entrance Expansion – Extracting Your Awareness from being collapsed inside the energy field of an identification, reaction or projection

    - To resolve identifications, expectations, projections, and reactions created by the ego

- WAIT – Waiting Accesses Intuitive Truth - Waiting for Clarity

    - During the waiting you fully feel whatever is there – using CORE, SEE and GPS

    - This process clears the barriers to Knowing

- CORE – Center of Remaining Energy - Feeling into the Core of the Feeling

    - Feeling into the Core of the Feeling of the fear of not existing

    - Feeling into the Core of the Feeling of being driven or reactive

    - Feeling into the Core of the Feeling of being rebellious, victimized or isolated

- WONDER – Wait On Neutral During Emotional Reactions - Unplugging the Power/Shifting to Neutral

    - To be applied to habits of reactivity

- **When this Dynamic is Absent**

    - I get the sense of myself from the essential nature of who I truly am rather then from ideas/definitions of who I think I am

Barrier 10
The Conditioning of Dogma

- **The Core Dynamic**
  - Excluding Other Perspectives

- **The Feeling Level Decision**
  - I am my perspective
  - If I have to change the way I see things, I will lose the sense of who I am

- **The Conditioned Response**
  - My way or the highway
  - I'm right and others are wrong

- **Knowing the Distinction between**
  - Perspective and Identity

- **What needs to be learned?**
  - To have the experience of Pure Awareness as the nature of who you really are so that you come out of the illusion that what you are is defined by your perspective
  - That you are pure awareness and not your perspective

- **What needs to be optimized?**
  - Your receptivity to learning new things
  - To be so established in the experience of Pure Awareness as your essential nature that you are naturally open to see things in new ways without having it disrupt your sense of who you are

- **The Pure Awareness Techniques**

  - GAP – Greater Awareness Place - Experiencing Pure Awareness in the Gap Between Thoughts

    - To provide the direct experience of what you really are

  - AGAPE – Accessing Greater Awareness Place Everywhere - Experiencing Pure
    Awareness Everywhere

    - To provide the direct experience of your oneness with everything

    - To provide the direct experience of the place that Knowing comes from

  - SEE – Side Entrance Expansion – Extracting Your Awareness from being collapsed inside the energy field of an identification, reaction or projection

    - To resolve identifications, expectations, projections, and reactions created by the ego

  - WAIT – Waiting Accesses Intuitive Truth - Waiting for Clarity

    - During the waiting you fully feel whatever is there – using CORE, SEE and GPS

    - This process clears the barriers to Knowing

  - CORE – Center of Remaining Energy - Feeling into the Core of the Feeling

    - Feeling into the Core of the Feeling of the fear of being influenced

    - Feeling into the Core of the Feeling of fear of losing your identity

- Feeling into the Core of the Feeling of the fear of being ostracized for being different from your tribe
- SANYAMA – Silent Awareness Notices Your Answers Manifesting Automatically
  - To get the basis of your decisions from within yourself rather than from a perspective that you have been taught
- WONDER – Wait On Neutral During Emotional Reactions - Unplugging the Power/Shifting to Neutral
  - To be applied to habits of being dogmatic or rigid in your perspective
- **When this Dynamic is Absent**
  - I know things from deep within myself and I know the difference between thinking and knowing

Barrier 11
The Conditioning of Misinterpretation

- **The Core Dynamic**
  - Manufacturing Interpretations
- **The Feeling Level Decision**
  - I am my stories
  - If I have to change my stories, who will I be?
- **The Conditioned Response**
  - To live inside of the interpretations of events rather than live in the reality of the present moment

- **Knowing the Distinction between**
  - Events and Interpretations

- **What needs to be learned?**
  - How to live in reality instead of a fantasy
  - That you are pure awareness and not your stories
  - The clear distinction between knowing and attachment to emotionally based stories

- **What needs to be optimized?**
  - Your ability to deal with things as they are

- **The Pure Awareness Techniques**
  - GAP – Greater Awareness Place - Experiencing Pure Awareness in the Gap Between Thoughts
    - To provide the direct experience of what you really are
  - AGAPE – Accessing Greater Awareness Place Everywhere - Experiencing Pure Awareness Everywhere
    - To provide the direct experience that you are the Universe
    - To provide the direct experience of the place that Knowing comes from
  - SEE – Side Entrance Expansion – Extracting Your Awareness from being collapsed inside the energy field of an identification, reaction or projection
    - To resolve identifications, expectations, projections, and reactions created by the ego
    - WAIT – Waiting Accesses Intuitive Truth - Waiting for Clarity

- During the waiting you fully feel whatever is there – using CORE, SEE and GPS

- This process clears the barriers to Knowing

- CORE – Center of Remaining Energy - Feeling into the Core of the Feeling

  - Feeling into the Core of the Feeling of the fear of not having an opinion

  - Feeling into the Core of the Feeling of fear of life being meaningless

  - Feeling into the Core of the Feeling of that what happened is less than perfect

  - Feeling into the Core of the Feeling of the fear of being different than your parents

- WONDER – Wait On Neutral During Emotional Reactions - Unplugging the Power/Shifting to Neutral

  - To be applied to the habit of needing to create meaning

  - To be applied to the habit of needing to understand with your intellect

- **When this Dynamic is Absent**

  - I sense the perfection of everything even when my intellect doesn't get it appendix | the essence of each core dynamic

Barrier 12
The Conditioning of Reactivity

- **The Core Dynamic**
  - Over-reacting to Circumstances

- **The Feeling Level Decision**
  - To be accepted I'll behave like those around me
  - Being reactive is the way to be

- **The Conditioned Response**
  - To take action out of emotional reactions
  - To be impulsive

- **Knowing the Distinction between**
  - Feeling your feelings fully and being over-reactive

- **What needs to be learned?**
  - How to keep your cool when it's the most difficult
  - How to maintain equanimity in pleasure or pain
  - That you are Pure Awareness and not your emotions or reactions

- **What needs to be optimized?**
  - The sense of yourself as Pure Awareness distinct from your reactions
  - Equanimity and Peace of Mind

- **The Pure Awareness Techniques**
  - SEE – Side Entrance Expansion – Extracting Your Awareness from being collapsed inside the energy field of your reactions

- To resolve reactions to unmet expectations

- WAIT – Waiting Accesses Intuitive Truth - Waiting for Clarity

  - During the waiting you fully feel whatever is there – including the tendency to be reactive - using CORE, SEE and GPS

  - To wait rather than be reactive or impulsive

- CORE – Center of Remaining Energy - Feeling into the Core of the Feeling

  - Feeling into the Core of the Feelings that drive the emotional reactions

- WONDER – Wait On Neutral During Emotional Reactions - Unplugging the Power/Shifting to Neutral

  - To be applied to the habits of inappropriate emotional reactions

  - To break the habit of reacting instead of waiting and feeling

- **When this Dynamic is Absent**

  - I feel a deep sense of equanimity even during experiences of pain or pleasure